BLESSED ARE
the BALANCED

A Seminarian's Guide
to Following Jesus
in the Academy

BLESSED ARE
the BALANCED

A Seminarian's Guide
to Following Jesus
in the Academy

Paul E. Pettit
R. Todd Mangum

Kregel
Ministry

Blessed Are the Balanced: A Seminarian's Guide to Following Jesus in the Academy

© 2014 by Paul E. Pettit and R. Todd Mangum

Published by Kregel Publications, a division of Kregel, Inc., P.O. Box 2607, Grand Rapids, MI 49501.

The Greek font GraecaU and the Hebrew font New JerusalemU are both available from www.linguistsoftware.com/lgku.htm, +1-425-775-1130.

All Scripture quotations, unless otherwise indicated, are from the NEW AMERICAN STANDARD BIBLE®. Copyright © 1960, 1962, 1963, 1968, 1971, 1972, 1973, 1975, 1977 by The Lockman Foundation. Used by permission. (www.Lockman.org)

ISBN 978-0-8254-4345-9

Printed in the United States of America
14 15 16 17 18 / 5 4 3 2 1

CONTENTS

INTRODUCTION

Loving God While Learning about God

Attending a seminary is an exciting experience. You study the Bible in detail. You engage in theological discussions. You learn how to minister in various contexts. You study how to reach and teach people in various age-groups. You learn how to communicate the Bible to others by teaching, preaching, and counseling.

Also you are surrounded by Christians who, like you, are dedicated to serving the Lord faithfully. You are stimulated spiritually in chapel services, in small-group settings, in prayer meetings, and in daily devotional times. And you have opportunities for sharing God's truths with others.

Yes, seminary can be a stimulating experience and a soul-enriching time. But it can also be dangerous. Seminary, believe it or not, can be hazardous to your spiritual health. With almost daily exposure to God's Word, it is easy to become spiritually cold.

Unfortunately a good number of students graduate with a head full of biblical and doctrinal knowledge, but with a heart that has grown cold to God. They enter seminary eager to know God better, but in their seminary years they become callous toward spiritual things. You would think that a few years of seminary training would deepen their walk with God, encourage their spiritual growth, and enhance their desire for spiritual things.

But this does not always happen. Why? What causes spiritual burnout among seminary students? Why is a seminary education detrimental to your spiritual health? Why is it difficult to learn about God and adore Him at the same time?

Many factors can contribute to this problem. And this book helps explain how to avoid some of the common pitfalls that can lead to spiritual burnout when one enters into an academic study of God and the Scriptures. This work encourages a healthy balance between knowledge and experience; between faith and learning.

The English Standard Version of 1 Corinthians 8:1 reads, "knowledge puffs up." When you read those words can you picture a bloated, oversized, student? The apostle Paul explains that charity or love builds up, but he warns that much learning carries with it the temptation for one to think more highly of himself than he ought. Again there is a difference between second-hand acquired knowledge and firsthand lived-out wisdom.

More than one veteran of theological higher education has warned that learning that stays in the head becomes cold and stagnant, but truth that makes its way to the heart is warm and vibrant. But how does this happen? Are there steps you can take to avoid becoming "puffed up" in this potentially risky process? How do you integrate head and heart knowledge?

This book focuses on how students of God and the Scriptures can achieve a healthy balance between both rigorous academic scholarship and a growing piety. Put another way, in the pages that follow you will learn how students, church leaders, Bible study group members, and Christian teachers can sidestep burnout, apathy, or a growing hard heart. You will learn how to avoid the process of the Bible becoming no more than an academic text. Sometimes intense seasons of study may lead to a hardening of your spiritual arteries, but there are time-tested principles and practices that can keep your heart soft for the fellowship of God and His people.

We all know friends who started out in a pursuit of advanced Bible study with the best of intentions but were sidelined for various reasons. Often they explain, "Seminary became for me a dry desert, and the Bible lost its appeal as I came to view it as one more assignment to check off my list!"

Our goal is that a fresh wind of the Spirit will guide you into a balanced approach to healthy spirituality and rigorous scholarship. Many readers in various ministry endeavors have devoted their entire vocational lives to the Scriptures, and they seem to grow more in love with its precious pages each day. How do they walk the tight rope between critical scholarship and a vibrant faith?

One seminary founder clarified the problem by stating, "You can make the Scriptures as clear as ice, but just as cold!" He often warned students to avoid the danger of what he called spiritual frostbite. We seek to do the same.

One of the main sources of frustration for serious students is a growing gap between acquisition of knowledge and the experience of internalizing or living out the knowledge they have accumulated. The new facts may exist in the head, but often in the journey from head to heart much is lost in translation. Malcolm Warford nicely summarizes this potential problem.

While the earliest classical philosophical tradition understood knowing as lived experience rather than abstract thought, the Sophists created the school as the primary place for learning. The earlier emphasis on learning that occurs by formation in a community's life—its values, institutional practices, and traditions—was superseded by teaching and learning in the formal setting of the school. Ever since, we have struggled with reconnecting knowledge and experience in the kind of practical wisdom that shapes our souls and forms the practices of our lives.[1]

Four Warning Signs of a Shaky Balance

Zealous students need to watch for four warning signs as they embark on a seminary education. *The first is confusing your identity* in Christ with your identity as a vocational pastor, Bible teacher, or theologian. Much like the thrill of starting out on a long hike, the journey of Christian scholarship begins by everything seeming to be exciting, new, and fresh. The sacred Scriptures come alive with initial Hebrew and Greek language studies. Difficult theological concepts are broken down into understandable categories by gifted teachers and exciting classroom lectures. And the end result of all this new study is often a growing, vibrant faith.

However, over time a student can easily confuse his identity *in* Christ with his identity as one who learns and teaches *about* Christ. The new student may soon replace his passion for reading and understanding the Bible with damaging zeal for de-

---

1   Malcolm L. Warford, ed., *Practical Wisdom: On Theological Teaching and Learning* (New York: Peter Lang, 2004), 11.

fending his own narrowing stance or fringe doctrinal position regarding the Bible. Instead of viewing the Bible as the fresh font of spiritual nurture, the advancing student uses the Bible as a weapon for fighting theological battles.

We are to worship Christ, not the book that shows us Christ. We are commanded to point others to life in Christ—not life in the academic study of Christ. Making the Bible an academic textbook can be a trap, for it can divert us from the life-giving power it offers. Sadly, sometimes Christian academic experts vehemently argue, sometimes with seething anger, over certain passages of Scripture, seeking to defend their position, while at the same time denying by their very actions the love of God those same passages advocate! Thomas à Kempis captured this point well:

> What good does it do you if you dispute loftily about the Trinity, but lack humility and therefore displease the Trinity? It is not lofty words that make you righteous or holy or dear to God. . . . I would much rather *experience* contrition than be able to give a definition of it. . . . Naturally, everyone wants knowledge. But what good is knowledge without the fear of God? A humble peasant who serves God is much more pleasing to him than an arrogant academic. . . . Learned people always want their wisdom to be noticed and recognized.[2]

When one's very own identity gets so wrapped up in whether he holds a certain doctrine or denominational creedal point, dan-

---

2   Thomas á Kempis in *The Christian Theology Reader*, 2d ed., ed. Alister McGrath (Malden, MA: Blackwell, 2001), 211.

ger looms on the horizon. Our identity should rest securely in Christ, not in the various positions we hold. Mixing our identity with our success or failure as a minister, theologian, or biblical scholar is not worth the high price exacted from the effort.

Our goal should be to love Christ always. And we should love the members of the church and show reverence toward the Bible and the One who gave us the Scriptures. Keeping and maintaining this healthy balance requires diligence.

Some Christian academicians reveal that they love their views on Christ more than they love Christ. They demonstrate passion for debates over the Scriptures more than passion for the Scriptures themselves. They long to argue about the church more than they long to be with the members and Head of the church. Keeping your identity focused solely on Christ and Him alone will help you stay balanced in your theological studies. But how do you keep close tabs on your identity? This book shows you how.

The *second* warning sign is a growing *isolation and privatization* in your academic studies. Often the deeper one delves into a study of theology or the Bible the more isolated and private one becomes. At the outset, the eager student attends a variety of Bible studies and prayer meetings with various fellow believers. The fellowship seems fresh and inviting, and there is a growing identification with Christians from various backgrounds. And yet over time isolation and individualization can creep in and as a result, the advanced student believes only his or her set of beliefs is the correct one. A hardening of the spiritual arteries occurs and brings narrowness and suspicion, even doctrinal paranoia.

This second warning serves as an encouragement for you as a new seminary student to spend significant portions of time with a variety of mature believers. True, your heartfelt convictions and well-developed beliefs should be firmly held. However, seek to avoid becoming rigid and unbending in your beliefs and doctrines. The danger of isolation, privatization, and individualization is a looming threat in any undertaking of biblical and theological study.

Time spent with others in theological reflection is critical. New students should share with trusted friends what, why, and how they are learning. We all need others in the body of Christ to check on us to see how we are progressing. We need others who love us enough to ask us tough questions about the doubts we may experience. We need to surround ourselves in conversation with mature believers when we study "difficult passages" or try to comprehend the depths of justice and mercy of our holy God. Often the "mysteries" of theology and biblical study shake the very foundations of our faith; thus we need to interact intensely with faith-filled friends who have journeyed along a similar path and emerged stronger from the study.

A *third* warning sign in your theological higher education is *a lack of zeal and service for God* and others. Serious study of the Bible and theology should lead to ever-increasing levels of love for God and service to His people. Along with stimulating academic study and rigorous intellectual intake, there needs to be a corresponding level of humble output and serious service. We learn in order to live, not the other way around. Be careful when you notice an increasing lack of zeal and service for God and others. This could mean you are missing out on the balance that leads to blessing.

A *fourth* sign of an academic downslide is a *lack of time for prayer and reflection*. Psalm 1:2 reminds us there are really only two times when we need to meditate on the Word of God: day and night. And yet, during seasons of intense study we often fail to take adequate time to reflect on what we are learning. Prayer can become perfunctory and lifeless. We become so busy acquiring knowledge that we no longer take time to contemplate *what* we are learning and *how* the new learning can be integrated into our lives.

The enemy of our souls uses the legitimate doubts we experience to drive a wedge between our heads and our hearts. His tactics have not changed since the garden of Eden. He isolated Eve and cunningly asked, "Has God said?" (Gen. 3:1). Obviously Eve should have prayed to God, reflected on what He really said, and asked Adam, her friend and husband for faith-filling advice. And yet in her isolation and doubt she questioned the goodness of God. The problem with increasing levels of Christian privatization is that it leads to further isolation. Instead of building deeper associations in the body of Christ, we further alienate ourselves. As we study, we need to pray. When we learn, we need to reflect. While we are struggling with understanding who God is, we must at the same time remember what He has done!

We must continually strive for balance between a humble pursuit of godly wisdom and an insatiable appetite for acquiring theological knowledge. The former ought to produce a warm, vibrant relationship with God, while an overemphasis on the latter often induces a cold, doubting introspective lifestyle that can lead to extended seasons of habitual doubt and selfishness. As Jesus promised, "I came that they may have *life*" (John 10:10).

Introduction

	CHECKLIST OF AN UNBALANCED ACADEMIC CHRISTIAN LIFE
1.	A confusion regarding one's identity in Christ with an identity as a worker for Christ. Thinking, "Unless I win this theological argument, I am not important." Are you secure in Christ alone? Are you secure in the work you do for Christ or the study you undertake about Christ?
2.	An increasing amount of isolation and privatization. Thinking, "There are really only a handful of us true believers, and I worry about some of them. I should get out of my study and interact with others, but I guess I'm the intellectual type." Are you surrounded by a handful of faithful, authentic friends who know you well?
3.	A decreasing amount of service toward God and others in the body. Thinking, "I should probably balance my study time with service or outreach, but I need more knowledge to make certain I'm correct in my positions. I don't have time to serve others; I'm studying and researching to find real answers. Are you engaged in selfless service? Why or why not?

CHECKLIST OF AN UNBALANCED ACADEMIC CHRISTIAN LIFE	
4.	A lack of prayer and meditative reflection. Thinking, "I should probably set aside time for authentic prayer and honest contemplation, but I have all these increasing academic deadlines that I must fulfill!" Or, "I need to meditate on Scripture, but I want to learn what this new church controversy is all about first." Do you always need to be with others? Why?

Chapter 1

CHRISTIAN MATURITY AND HIGHER EDUCATION

Can They Be Balanced?

Consider these two scenarios. Lingering at the moving truck's sliding back door while glancing at old correspondence, Tyler somberly reflected on being so excited at receiving his acceptance letter to seminary. He had envisioned late nights with friends studying the classic theologians of the faith. He longed to know more about the *content* of his faith, the *reasons* he should believe, the underlying *nature* of his faith. He desired to dig deeper. He wondered why, in just two brief semesters, he now struggled with deepening levels of doubt. He was confused as to why he had become so cynical and sarcastic toward the faith he once held dear. Tyler entered with such eager anticipation and was now leaving with little enlightenment and certainly no degree in hand.

When I (Paul) was in grade school I enjoyed most subjects. Reading, writing, and arithmetic all held my interest. Growing up in northeast Kansas the fall months seamlessly turned to winter and normally a blanket of snow covered the school parking lot and playground. Then spring would arrive in its full splendor. Like suddenly awakened flowers shooting up from their long-dormant positions under the cold soil, all the kids in my class sprang from our assigned seats and raced to the playground.

Plenty of options existed from which to choose. There were the swing sets, monkey bars, merry-go-rounds, and jungle gyms. But one piece of playground equipment always captured my imagination more than the others. I was always drawn to and intrigued by the teeter-totter. Simple in design, this playground staple consisted of one long piece of lumber bolted atop a sturdy metal bar. But oh, the potential dangers lurking; for a group of young boys they seemed endless.

The normal way to ride on the teeter-totter was for one child to sit on one end of the long board and a similar-sized child to sit on the opposing end of the board. While we pushed off with our feet and legs, the up-and-down motion provided hours of endless fun.

But hilarity followed when different-sized kids would try to keep one end of the board suspended in the air. Or two or more kids would try to launch one child into the air. And especially dangerous was to quickly run up the teeter-totter and then to the metal bar; keeping one foot on one side of the bar and another foot on the other side. As weight was slightly shifted from one side to the other, the final goal of *balancing* the teeter-totter could be achieved. This took skill, patience, experience, and wisdom. Too much weight in one direction always produced a painful and embarrassing spill.

Students also need to exercise extreme caution in order to balance growth in Christ (a life-long pursuit of spiritual maturity) with a concentrated effort at learning more about God (undertaking a course of Christian study or pursuit of theology).

Surely the desire to accomplish this task is a worthy goal. Scripture always emphasizes the holistic nature of man. For example, Jesus answered an expert in the Law by referring to Deuteronomy 6:5, pointing out that believers should love God with all of their being; heart, soul, strength, and *mind*. In addition, Peter advised his readers to know the *reasons* why they believe. He urged them to "sanctify Christ as Lord in your hearts, always being ready to *make a defense* to everyone who asks you to give an account for the hope that is in you, yet with gentleness and reverence" (1 Peter 3:15).

Those who desire to learn more about God long for a good thing. Today the church has been accused of "dumbing down the gospel," and some say that the technical and digital revolution means we are "amusing ourselves to death."[1] Now more than ever, we need theologians who can learn and defend the orthodox doctrines of the faith. The church desperately needs vigorous defenders who can engage a lost and broken post-Christian culture.

In addition, evangelicalism is in need of those who burn with passion for following Jesus Christ. The church is looking for sold-out disciple-makers who mirror the commitment of Jesus and His earliest followers. Possessing a head full of facts and dogmas without a heart filled with love for Jesus and a passion to serve the Savior is of little value.

But how can this teeter totter between Christian maturity and a seminary education be mastered? Can one really possess both a mind able to defend the faith and a heart passionately beating for Christ? To tiptoe up one side of this teeter-totter and peek over the edge, several terms must be defined.

---

1   Neil Postman. *Amusing Ourselves to Death: Public Discourse in the Age of Show Business* (New York: Penguin, 1985), 155.

Chapter 1

What Is Christian Maturity?

The New Testament writers employed several metaphors to describe the process and product of growth in Christ. The following are three of them. First, the apostle Paul used the metaphor of a *grown man*, urging Jesus' followers to *grow up* in "the body of Christ, until we all attain to the unity of the faith, and of the knowledge of the Son of God, to a *mature man*, [attaining] to the measure of the stature which belongs to the fullness of Christ [so that] we are no longer to be children" (Eph. 4:12-14, italics added).

Paul fought against his prevailing culture (which was filled with various private religions and individualized beliefs) by showing new believers that theirs was a religion of growth toward unity. Each person was needed, and all were encouraged to give and contribute their unique faith gift to the church in order for the church to become a *mature* man. Are you maturing in your Christian faith?

Second, Jesus used the illustration of good *fruit* to show results of growth in the Christian life. He said, "You will know them by their fruits. Grapes are not gathered from thorn bushes nor figs from thistles, are they? So every good tree bears good fruit, but the bad tree bears bad fruit. A good tree cannot produce bad fruit, nor can a bad tree produce good fruit...So then, you will know them by their fruits" (Matt. 7: 16-18, 20). Are you producing good fruit as a result of following Jesus?

Third, John used the image of *light* to describe maturing in faith. John admonished, "But if we walk in the Light as He Himself is in the Light, we have fellowship with one another" (1 John 1:7). And Paul similarly encouraged his Ephesian readers, "For you were formerly darkness, but now you are Light in the

Lord; walk as children of Light" (Eph. 5:8). Are you avoiding the darkness and walking in the light?

These three metaphors (growing, producing, and walking) represent what it means to become spiritually mature. Maturity in Christ means (a) putting away childish things and becoming an *adult* in Christ, (b) partnering with the Holy Spirit to produce *good fruit*, and (c) walking in the *light* of God's truths. The Scriptures view Christian maturity as normative for believers. Living things grow. But can growth in Christ occur when a person undertakes an advanced study in theology? Is it possible to see growth in Christ *alongside* rigorous academic achievement? Can these two be balanced in a healthy manner?

What Is "Higher Education?"

Some Christian leaders have discouraged advanced biblical or theological study. And some Christian denominations look with disdain on pursuing higher education.[2] On the other hand, the Council for Christian Colleges and Universities (CCCU) holds as its mission statement, "To advance the cause of Christ-centered higher education and to help our institutions transform lives by faithfully relating scholarship and service to biblical truth."[3]

---

2   Brethren leader James Taylor Jr. tolerated post-secondary education, while James Harvey Symington strongly discouraged it. Toward the end of his life, Symington actively suppressed any discussion that found value in higher education (http://56755.blogspot.com/2009/03/brethren-revisited.html). In addition, Amish and some Mennonites discourage study in higher education (http://www.guidedbiblestudies.com/library/christianbrethren.htm).

3   Council for Christian Colleges and Universities, (http://www.cccu.org/about, under the heading Mission).

Chapter 1

In the Western world advanced education is primarily viewed as post-secondary education ("graduate school" or "further education") undertaken on a voluntary basis. This can mean studying at a university or a seminary, taking a certificate class at a local junior or community college, or attending a vocational or trade school. The Platonic Academy was founded in the fourth century BC and included theological discussion as a part of its course of study.[4] Modern universities (a collection of more than one "college") grew out of the monastic tradition in which individuals felt "called by God" to devote themselves solely to the church. Universities therefore trained members to become officers and leaders in the church.

In the Middle Ages, theology was considered the "ultimate subject" at universities and was referred to as "Queen of the Sciences." The word *theology* comes from the Greek θεολογία which combines θεός (*theos,* "God") and λογία (*logia,* "study of"). Theology was taught first. Then the Trivium (the "three ways" or "three roads")—grammar, logic, rhetoric—were taught. After the Trivium was mastered, students studied the Quadrivium (the "four ways, or "four roads"): arithmetic, geometry, music, and astronomy. Additional subjects, such as philosophy, existed primarily to assist with the undertaking of theological thought.[5]

Over the centuries, however, theology's valued position as "queen" began to erode. During the Enlightenment era especially, people questioned whether faith and reason could exist together. Surely one could be held, but could both? Debates broke

---

4   John Dillon, *The Heirs of Plato: A Study in the Old Academy, 347~274 BC* (Oxford: Oxford University Press, 2003) 2.

5   Thomas Albert Howard, *Protestant Theology and the Making of the Modern German University* (Oxford: Oxford University Press, 2006), 56.

out as to whether the study of theology was an undertaking in science or theory? Later in the United States, universities such as Harvard, Yale, and Princeton were founded with the distinct goal of providing theological training for clergy.[6]

Is Balance Possible?

Now that we have taken these brief looks into Christian maturity and higher education as separate entities, we return to our original question: Can a healthy pursuit of *both* of these targets be achieved? How can a balance occur? Can you really stand in the middle of the teeter-totter as a whole person who is passionate about Christian formation and deeply engaged in advanced academic pursuits?

The answer to the question is a resounding *yes*. However, you must adhere to certain principles, guidelines, and warnings, for the journey to become a success.

J. Gresham Machen described this dilemma as a potential conflict between Christianity and culture.

> "Are then Christianity and culture in a conflict that is to be settled only by the destruction of one or the other of the contending forces? A...solution fortunately, is possible—namely, consecration. Instead of destroying the arts and sciences or being indifferent to them, let us cultivate them with all the enthusiasm of the veriest humanist, but at the

---

6   George M. Marsden, *The Soul of the American University: From Protestant Establishment to Established Nonbelief* (New York: Oxford University Press, 1994), 41.

same time consecrate them to the service of our God. Instead of stifling the pleasures afforded by the acquisition of knowledge or by the appreciation of what is beautiful, let us accept these pleasures as the gifts of a heavenly Father. Instead of obliterating the distinction between the Kingdom and the world, or on the other hand withdrawing from the world into a sort of modernized intellectual monasticism, let us go forth joyfully, enthusiastically to make the world subject to God."[7]

The Dangers Involved in Failing to Achieve Balance

Someone may argue, "What difference does it make if I'm not involved in either of these pursuits." All Christians are called to grow. And all Christians are called to know what they believe. As stated earlier, we are always to be "ready to make a defense to everyone who asks you to give an account for the hope that is in you, yet with gentleness and reverence" (1 Pet. 3:15). So both of these goals are more than simply worthwhile attainments; they are scriptural mandates. Think of these two arenas of development as the two ends of our teeter-tooter example.

On one far end stands the believer who does not see the benefit of learning about the content of his or her faith. Because he does not see the importance of learning "sound doctrine," he is in danger of being led astray by false teaching. As Paul warned, "As a result, we are no longer to be children, tossed here and there by waves and carried about by every wind of doctrine, by

---

7   D.G. Hart, *J. Gresham Machen: Selected Shorter Writings* (Phillipsburg: P & R Publishing, 2004), 402.

the trickery of men, by craftiness in deceitful scheming" (Eph. 4:14). All Christians should "be diligent to present yourself approved to God as a workman who does not need to be ashamed, accurately handling the word of truth" (2 Tim. 2:15). Believers need to understand *why* they believe *what* they believe.

On the other end of the teeter-totter stands the believer who slips into the practice of always studying and learning but fails to *practice* or *implement* what he is learning. This subtle danger can creep in unawares. As James warned his readers, "But prove yourselves doers of the word, and not merely hearers who delude themselves. For if anyone is a hearer of the word and not a doer, he is like a man who looks at his natural face in a mirror; for once he has looked at himself and gone away, he has immediately forgotten what kind of person he was" (James 1:22-24).

After much biblical or theological study, some may tend to think proudly, "I know so much more than most Christians," or "I am smarter than the average Christ-follower." How strange that the advanced study of a book promoting humility and service toward others would leave one feeling smug over his knowledge or ability to recall biblical data or doctrinal facts.

Understanding the Inherent Imperfections in All Theological Systems

God has made Himself known through revelation. Theologians distinguish between general and special revelation. General revelation holds that God's existence and attributes can be known by all through both an internal sensing and by external observation and discovery of nature, the universe, and even historical events. Special revelation refers to the distinct self-disclosure of God to specific persons and ultimately through Scripture. Christian maturity and academic theological study, which are to be held in balance, can be addressed by these two categories of revelation.

Because of the gift of general revelation, mankind can observe the world as it is. From the intricacies of nature, the complexities of the human body, and the wonder of beauty and art, people can reason there must be a Creator. The apostle Paul explained this concept clearly: "For the wrath of God is revealed from heaven against all ungodliness and unrighteousness of men who suppress the truth in unrighteousness, because that which is known about God is evident within them; for God made it evident to them. For since the creation of the world His invisible attributes, His eternal power and divine nature, have been clearly seen, being understood through what has been made, so that they are without excuse" (Rom. 1:18-20).

All theological systems are man-made and therefore inherently flawed to some degree. Of course they contain truth, but they are not *the* truth like the Scriptures. The Bible is the inspired and inerrant Word of God. As Paul wrote, "All Scripture is inspired by God [lit., God-breathed] and profitable for teaching, for reproof, for correction, for training in righteousness" (2 Tim. 3:16). Inspiration can be defined as the work of the Holy Spirit in enabling the human authors to record what God wanted written down. The writing of the Scriptures was divinely guided. Inerrancy means that the Bible is trustworthy and reliable. And because the Scriptures are authoritative, they can be referred to as God's Word.

Christian maturity is ultimately based on both the general and special revelation of God. The special revelation of God speaks to the mystery of salvation (right relationship with God). For example, the apostle Paul told the Corinthian believers, "We speak God's wisdom in a mystery, the hidden wisdom which

God predestined before the ages to our glory" (1 Cor. 2:7). The special revelation of God describes the process of sanctification (right fellowship with God). The following passages all mention how God sanctifies (sets apart for service) His own:

> "For we are His workmanship, created in Christ Jesus for good works, which God prepared beforehand so that we would walk in them" (Eph. 2:10).

> "For I am confident of this very thing, that He who began a good work in you will perfect it until the day of Christ Jesus" (Phil. 1:6).

> "For it is God who is at work in you, both to will and to work for His good pleasure" (Phil. 2:13).

> "But we should always give thanks to God for you, brethren beloved by the Lord, because God has chosen you from the beginning for salvation through sanctification by the Spirit and faith in the truth" (2 Thess. 2:13).

These passages show that God is at work in the lives of believers to bring them more and more into conformity to Christ. Sanctification is both an accomplished fact and a process of growth. We are formed and ever forming. To use the metaphors mentioned above, we are *growing up* into our full stature, we are producing *good fruit* that benefits the body of Christ, and we are learning to *walk in the light*, as more and more light is revealed to us. Special revelation shows how the process of sanctification should occur. But we rely on general revelation as well. We tap into the wisdom of saints who have gone before us to learn some of the "best practices" for growing in godliness.

We look to learned men and women of the faith who have studied the Scriptures and systematized their observations into reasonable divisions of learning. Believers today rely on (a) the insights and knowledge of Christians who lived in previous ages, (b) doctrines and dogmas formulated through church councils, (c) popular and academic writings on the faith, and (d) faith practices and patterns from others who have embraced Christ as Lord.

Humans were created as moral agents. We were gifted with the incredible power of choice. A glimpse into a Garden of Eden scene reveals, "The LORD God commanded the man, saying, 'From any tree of the garden you may eat freely," (Gen. 2:16). However, even though humans have been granted this amazing freedom to choose, we are ultimately still frail, weak, and finite. The following Bible passages address this weakness.

> "Can you discover the depths of God? Can you discover the limits of the Almighty? They are high as the heavens, what can you do? Deeper than Sheol, what can you know? Its measure is longer than the earth and broader than the sea" (Job 11:7-9).

> "When I consider Your heavens, the work of Your fingers, the moon and the stars, which You have ordained; what is man that You take thought of him, and the son of man that You care for him?" (Ps. 8:3-4).

> "LORD, make me to know my end and what is the extent of my days; let me know how transient I am.

Behold, you have made my days as handbreadths, and my lifetime as nothing in Your sight; surely every man at his best is a mere breath" (Ps. 39:4-5).

"Such knowledge is too wonderful for me; it is too high, I cannot attain to it" (Ps.139:6).

"A voice says, "Call out." Then he answered, "What shall I call out?" All flesh is grass, and all its loveliness is like the flower of the field. The grass withers, the flower fades, when the breath of the LORD blows upon it; surely the people are grass. The grass withers, the flower fades, but the word of our God stands forever" (Isa.40:6-8).

"Yet we do speak wisdom among those who are mature; a wisdom, however, not of this age nor of the rulers of this age, who are passing away; but we speak God's wisdom in a mystery, the hidden wisdom which God predestined before the ages to our glory; the wisdom which none of the rulers of this age has understood; for if they had understood it they would not have crucified the Lord of glory" (1 Cor. 2:6-8).

Understanding the Inherent Imperfection of All Christian Formation Systems

Both general and special revelation help gifted and learned scholars build systematic theologies, which are useful for the church and her people. But since these systems are based on the writings of imperfect people, these systems of thought are not inspired or inerrant. In a similar manner, methods and plans for growth in godliness also contain imperfections.

Becoming more like Christ has been God's goal for His followers since Jesus first chose 12 followers and began the process of building His church. Since that time, Christians have relied on the revelation of God and their own human intellect to devise plans and strategies for growth. The earliest followers of Jesus employed the methods they learned from the first disciples including prayer, the sharing of all things in common, regularly meeting together to observe baptism and the Lord's meal, and other distinctly Christian practices.

Through the ages, various practices were added to these in an attempt to become more fully devoted disciples of Jesus. But these practices, habits, and patterns of devotion, all devised to help us become mature Christians, do not have a 100% guarantee of success.

We can surely employ these methods in good faith expecting desired results, but God produces the results. Jesus said, "The wind blows where it wishes and you hear the sound of it, but do not know where it comes from and where it is going" (John 3:8).

Balancing the Head and the Heart: It Can Happen!

God made man in His own image (Gen. 1:26) and part of that image is the gift of reason. Scripture reveals the wisdom of God, which differs from the ruminations of the most learned or brilliant human thinkers. C. S. Lewis is an example of an atheist who was drawn to faith over time. His mother, Florence, died when he was nine years old. His best friend, Paddy, died during World War I. And yet the subtle emotion that prompted Lewis to keep investigating Christianity was joy. Joy was Lewis' term for a stab of longing that unexpectedly welled up in him during moments of contemplation, such as listening to an opera or reading an ancient Norse tale.

In his book, *The Weight of Glory*, Lewis wrote that the yearning he experienced during those moments convinced him there was another existence beyond this world: "For they are not the thing itself; they are only the scent of a love we have not found, the echo of a tune we have not heard, news from a country we have never visited."[8] In Lewis, faith and reason found a comfortable home. His was a brilliant mind and by all accounts a heartfelt, genuine faith.

The psalmist asked, "Examine me, O LORD, and try me; test my mind כִּלְיָה (*kilyah*) and my heart לֵב (*leb*)" (Ps. 26:2). In Hebrew, כִּלְיָה stands for the motives or understanding (the mind) and לֵב stands for the affections or emotions (the heart). We can truly find the golden mean between our heart and our head; we can strive for the healthy, holistic lifestyle of a devoted walk with the Savior and the passionate pursuit of academic excellence. A blessed balance *is* possible!

We do not have to suffer from spiritual frostbite when we pursue advanced studies in theology or the Bible. Paul encouraged the Philippian believers by admonishing them to focus on the peace of God. "And the peace of God, which surpasses all comprehension, will guard your *hearts* and your *minds* in Christ Jesus" (Phil. 4:7, italics added). In the Greek language

---

8   John Blake, *Surprised by C. S. Lewis: Why His Popularity Endures.* CNN Belief Blog, Dec. 17, 2010; http://religion.blogs. cnn.com/2010/12/17/surprised-by-c-s-lewis-why-his-popularity-endures/?hpt=C2

kardia "heart" was considered the center of the body and thus the center of the spiritual life, while *noema* "head" stood for mental perception or thoughts. The apostle Paul placed these two seemingly disparate parts together and promised us that the incredible peace of God can guard (garrison) both our emotions (feelings) and our thoughts (mental choices).

The next chapter highlights some of the potential dangers inherent in acquiring knowledge. And, the remaining chapters help explain how we can maintain the head/heart balance described above. Rest assured, Christian maturity and theological higher education are both worthy and attainable pursuits.

Chapter 2

LEARNING ABOUT GOD AND LIVING FOR GOD

Why Good Doctrine and Good Training Do Not Always Make a Good Leader

Survey what the Bible says about gaining knowledge, and anyone engaged in ministerial education comes away with some important things to think about (compare Prov. 2:2-6 with 1 Cor. 8:1, for starters). The teaching of Scripture as a whole seems to be something like this: knowledge is a good thing, but it carries with it a hazard—the tendency to puff up in pride.

An old aphorism says, "Knowledge is power." But knowledge gained in pursuit of power is risky business.

If there is one thing that seminary provides well, it is an increase in knowledge. As an academic dean, I know the kind of rigors required by the state and by accrediting agencies to ensure that students paying for education are getting their money's worth in terms of credible scholarship, legitimacy of information, and value of subjects covered for occupational preparation. None of this is bad.

Furthermore, Scripture encourages the pursuit of knowledge—at least the good kind of knowledge, the kind that increases your wisdom, understanding, and discernment. The book of Proverbs especially emphasizes this theme. "Buy truth, and do not sell it, get wisdom and instruction and understanding" (Prov. 23:23). There may be no better commendation for the pursuit of a seminary education than Proverbs 23:23 (except perhaps Proverbs 4:4 [NIV]: "Wisdom is supreme; therefore get wisdom. Though it costs all you have, get understanding!"). And yet, Paul's concern that an increase in knowledge can threaten the (more important) increase in love (1 Cor. 8:1) has to get our attention.

Why does pursuit of knowledge have a warning label?

A Telling Exercise

How do you react to the idea of pursuing knowledge and the warnings just surveyed? Here are several responses that *could* be indicative of a larger pattern:

- This is so true. I see people who think they are so smart, all the time.

- This gives me a good idea for a sermon I'm preparing (or paper I'm writing or presentation I'm working on).

- Well, yeah; Scripture does encourage the cultivation of wisdom and knowledge, but that doesn't necessarily mean one should go to seminary.

- Are these verses listed above quoted in their proper context? Is Proverbs' use of דַּעַת the same as Paul's use of γνῶσις in 1 Corinthians?

- [Yawn. Eye roll.] So, is there a point to this?

What is your reaction to these statements? Is the knowledge you are gaining, is the education you are receiving, cultivating in you a learner's spirit or a critical spirit? Has your learning bred understanding and wisdom, or cynicism? Is your engagement with scriptural principles first and foremost for application to yourself, or has this become a tool of your trade, an instrument of your (vocational) ministry?

This book explores the various hazards and deficiencies of knowledge accumulation. Of course we recognize that reading a book that analyzes these cautions itself falls in the category of further knowledge accumulation.

There is danger in learning about God for the sake of increasing one's skill in one's vocation. The danger is unavoidable to an extent, so one must be alert to the danger's enticements. One toxic corrosive to the soul commonly found among those who ply God's Word for a living is hypocrisy.

Posturing and Hypocrisy

I (Todd) once took my wife to a couple's event at which I was the speaker; my assigned topic was keeping love alive in one's marriage. But we argued about the directions to the church all the way there.

It is not uncommon for those in ministry to experience such "discouraging ironies." I have a pastor friend who is sure that when he is most prepared for a Sunday morning sermon the probability increases that someone in his family will be running late for church or that the kids will bicker in the car during the ride there. He believes this is evidence of spiritual warfare, satanic sabotage. He may be right.

Ministers urge people to be obedient in some area only to find themselves, ironically, at that moment, not feeling very obedient themselves. Probably nothing in the ministry is as discouraging and wearying to the soul as this very real tension.

Many ministers suggest this is just one of the occupational challenges ministers simply need to get used to. In this very vein, Martin Luther told his protégé, Philipp Melanchthon, "Be a sinner and sin boldly, but believe and rejoice in Christ even more boldly." Luther, like many a Protestant sage after him, was concerned that young Philipp could take too much to heart the guilt he felt when preaching, admonishing, and exhorting others, knowing full well that he himself was guilty of some of the same sin he railed against.

My counsel would actually be different from Luther's in this matter. Hypocrisy is a potent poison; ministers need to be alert to its damage. Jesus likens the power and quality of hypocrisy to yeast in a lump of dough (Luke 12:1); its influence starts out small and seemingly insignificant, but if neglected it will slowly permeate the dough until the entire batch is filled with yeast. I believe if Jesus were teaching today, He might use as His illustration a malignant tumor. Cancer can kill. No one who has been diagnosed with cancer is nonchalant about making sure that any trace of malignancy is removed; radical surgery, followed by an extensive regimen of medications, or chemotherapy, and/or radiation will be undertaken to ensure that not a single cancer cell remains.

We should take the discovery of hypocrisy in ourselves no less seriously. At the same time, the expectation that the minister be a perfect model of what he preaches is unreasonable. Such an expectation provokes resentment, which in turn can prompt hypocritical posturing. That pattern will prove devastating to oneself, and to one's family, which is part of the reason why pastors' kids have such a "PK" reputation. Living in the fishbowl is hard enough on its own; living with hypocrisy, too, often takes them over the top into full rebellion, even if expressed only passively.

Prepare for this while you are still in seminary, knowing that, even before you begin teaching what you are learning, the increased study in God's Word and in exploring theological principles is already setting you on a pattern of either increased godliness or increased hypocrisy (or possibly both!). What to do?

First, repent and turn completely from what the Old Testament identifies as "high-handed sin" (Num. 15:30, sins committed בְּיָד רָמָה; that is, sins committed knowingly, willingly, "defiantly"). Two examples of this in the Old Testament involve infractions that, in themselves do not seem like that big a problem. One involves a person who cursed God after becoming angry in a fight (Lev. 24:10-23), and another involves a person who got a head start on his collection of firewood by gathering sticks on the Sabbath (Num. 15:32-36). In both cases God commanded that the person be stoned. Why so dire a punishment for such seemingly slight transgressions? Even by Old Testament standards this seems severe.

I suggest deliberate defiance is what made these sins so serious. That observation reinforces the point here; deliberate toleration of sinfulness in one's life is serious business. We can be thankful that today God provides restoration through repentance rather than permanent banishment or death for such. Still the gracious restoration offered to the repentant differs from nonchalant dismissal of known sin, as though sin is insignificant. Christians would do well to maintain a sense of urgency over deliberate sinning.

Pornography habits or other sexual addictions are found all too commonly among ministers. Sociological and psychological factors contribute to and intensify the temptations of addiction that can impact people who have livelihoods in which they practice or prepare for long hours in private to perform in brief spurts in public, a category that applies to ministers as well as singers, actors and performing artists.[1] Likewise if you are characterized by hot-temperedness or violence; or if your root motivation for pursuing ministry goals is financial gain or even simple prestige; if you have a private drug or alcohol habit; if you are harboring a grudge against another person (dead or alive); or if you are knowingly nursing any kind of habitual pattern that you know is displeasing to the Lord, it is *not* okay. You need to break from this pattern of sin in your life. If you need help, ranging from an accountability partner you trust (who can honestly hold you accountable), to a support group, to acquiring the services of a paid professional counselor, then get it. It is unhealthy for a minister or one preparing for ministry to continue practicing ministry while patterns of rebellion against God fester unaddressed in his or her private life. And not only is it unhealthy; it is wrong.

Jesus' observation that "from everyone who has been given much, much will be required" (Luke 12:48) takes on special application for teachers and ministers, which Jesus' brother James notes (James 3:1). Jesus' harshest words are against

---

1   Patrick Carnes, *Out of the Shadows: Understanding Sexual Addiction* (Center City, MN: Hazelden, 1983).

teachers, preachers, and ministers who are adept at telling others what God's Word demands of them, but who do not practice it themselves (e.g., see Matt. 23).

Likewise, Paul addressed the problem of hypocrisy.

> You, therefore, who teach another, do you not teach yourself? You who preach that one should not steal, do you steal? You who say that one should not commit adultery, do you commit adultery? You who abhor idols, do you rob temples? You who boast in the Law, through your breaking the Law, do you dishonor God? For "the name of God is blasphemed among the Gentiles because of you," just as it is written (Rom. 2:21-24).

Moreover, Paul observed that hypocrisy is the instrument by which the conscience is "seared . . . as with a branding iron" (1 Tim. 4:2). Ministers ought not be engaged in admonishing God's people to do one thing, while privately practicing the reverse. Eventually the conscience of the minister will become so callous that he or she becomes immune to hearing the very voice of the Spirit for which they are to be a vehicle to others.

Repent. And keep one's conscience tender. That is point one.

Second, consider just what posture to which you aspire. Do you want to be known to your community as the "holy one of God"? Do you want to be considered the biblical or theological authority? If so, these are dangerous ambitions.

Eventually something in your sinful nature will slip out of the veneer into public view. Or, there is going to be a question raised that you cannot answer. Then, what?

The "know-it-all," when confronted with a question he cannot answer must bluff an answer or evade the question. The omni-competent visionary, confronted with a viewpoint he has not considered, must respond with defensiveness, or reassert his original point even more strongly, or bluster about why the advantages of his original proposal outweigh any other considerations someone else might raise.

The best answer to all of the above is to drop the posturing aspiration (and repent). Many ministers promote the posture of holy agent, biblical authority, theological expert, or grand prophetic visionary. Behind all these postures is pride, or the desire for power and prestige.

Jesus said of the faith community's leaders of His day "they love to stand and pray in the synagogues and on the street corners, so that they may be seen by men" (Matt. 6:5), "and they love the place of honor at banquets, and the chief seats in the synagogues, and respectful greetings in the market places, and being called, Rabbi" [or, we may say "Reverend," "Pastor," "Dr.," "Professor"] (Matt. 23:6-7). Jesus noted these characteristics as a warning against hypocrisy.

Besides aggressive forms of posturing, passive-aggressive forms exist, too, and they are no better. They may be more insidious because they are more subtle, and can seem even pious. These are the postures of the "super humble," the souls who are just so sensitive of heart that they can hardly bear the thought of opposition to their own "always-godly, true and good" initiatives.

Hypocrisy chips away at one's credibility publicly and privately, and often is lethal to ministry. Once abject hypocrisy is discovered, it is difficult to ever recover fully one's credibility, or one's reputation.

Pride and Ambition, Vanity, and Insecurity

Ministers are called to lead and teachers are called to teach. Legitimate authority is inherent in these positions. The temptation to posture arises when the minister realizes that he or she is in some way unprepared to carry the mantle of authority associated with these positions. This sense of unpreparedness and unworthiness can actually be healthy and legitimate; some of the best of the biblical leaders experienced this sense of fear and trepidation; for example, Moses, Solomon, Elisha, Jeremiah, and Paul.

Some very good biblical leaders struggled at first with pride and presumption, with attraction to the power and position being primary motivators for their entering the ministry. Nevertheless God was still able to develop them, with some trial and work, into good, godly leaders whom He eventually used mightily. Uzziah and Hezekiah were kings of Israel who would fit this description. The "sons of thunder," James and John were disciples of Jesus who fit this description. They were willing to leave a lucrative fishing business to go into full-time vocational ministry; but they aspired to seats of authority to the right and to the left of the Messiah (with their mother intervening on their behalf at one point, "reminding" Jesus of what these two young corporate leaders had given up to serve as assistants in His administration—Matt. 20:20-28; Mark 10:35-45).

A great example of a presumptuous leader who was out to make a name for himself was Peter. Peter was always trying to show that he could outdo anyone else in commitment, faith, and insight. Yet he repeatedly tripped over himself. His aspirations exceeded his actual abilities. He found it impossible to maintain his pretense in demonstrable action. He wound up floundering in the water trying to demonstrate his great faith (Matt. 14:28-31). He was rebuked as often as he was commended for his excessive zeal (e.g., Mark 8:33).

After three years of intensive "seminary training" with Jesus, Peter was ready and willing to do great things for God. He expressed in pious protest that he was far too unworthy and humble to allow Jesus to wash his feet (John 13). Then when Peter got the point after Jesus' explanation, he went to the other extreme, "Well, if 'cleansing me' is what this is about, then cleanse me thoroughly, head, hands, and whole body, too." Later that night, Peter insisted louder than all the others that he would never deny the Lord; others Jesus may not be able to count on, but he would die first before he would ever fall away.

This was not just an idle claim, an empty boast, though this is how Peter is often portrayed. Peter had faith and zeal enough to try to take on all the Roman soldiers who came to arrest Jesus. Not much of a swordsman, apparently (it was not the high priest servant's ear he was aiming for), Peter was still willing to put action behind his words; it was not just empty talk.

The problem was *not* that Peter had no faith; he had faith, but not enough. He had boldness and loyalty to Christ, just not to the extent he claimed.

If we take ourselves back to the dynamics in the Upper Room earlier that night, we can imagine what lured Peter into taking postures that set him up for failure. All the disciples thought they were headed for coronation; Peter thought the Upper Room was essentially an interview context in which the apprentices of Jesus were being assessed for position placement in the kingdom (one of whom in the room had apparently already failed—"you're fired!").

No wonder they were arguing about who was the greatest. No wonder they all protested to Jesus that, regardless of what the others did, they would be loyal to the end. They may have suspected that they would have to engage in a fight with the Roman authorities, but none of them doubted they would win. For one thing, they knew the kind of supernatural power their leader could wield if things really got bad. Besides, plum positions require risk and sacrifice; no pain, no gain.

None of them imagined that Jesus would just cave, which is what they thought He did when He yielded to arrest without a fight. That was really the point that broke Peter. He was willing to fight; he would even throw the first punch to get the rumble started. But just surrender? That Peter did not bargain for. And to be rebuked, yet again, in front of everyone for mustering the courage to do what Jesus apparently just did not have the stomach for? That he could not take.

Later that night, the rooster's crowing must have hit Peter hard. The horrible turn of events over the last few hours was not some unforeseen interruption or derailing of the plan; this was the plan Jesus had in mind all along. Jesus even had the foresight to predict what Peter's role in it would be. Jesus knew Peter's real level of faith, commitment and courage.

Peter probably never regained the hubris of his "seminary days," when in that stage of apprenticeship he imagined himself to be the one who would outshine all his classmates in what he accomplished for Jesus. Oh, the greatness of kingdom contribution he would make. Oh, the courage he would evidence, the extraordinary sacrifice he would contribute. But oh, the glory and prestige and honor he would secure; and all for God. So the greatness of reputation he was engendering was all holy and pure, right?

Wrong. Peter had to be humbled to the core of his being to be cured of all that. So shaken was Peter's self-confidence by the time the rooster crowed that it took a special post-Resurrection visit from Jesus to restore him so he could minister again.

And this is the point here. In Scripture a number of people were motivated by pride—people who postured before the public with great pretense to win for themselves the honor and prestige they coveted, yet people whom God still used to do significant things for Him. Consistently, though, He severely humbled them in the process. The lesson is clear. Better to "humble yourselves in the eyes of the Lord" than have Him do it. He is very good at humbling, and His ways of accomplishing it are effective; but they are never very pleasant for the one so humbled.

We also have an example or two in Scripture on the other end of the scale, of those who are called in a state of meekness and humility, but who end up *not* making great leaders. Gideon ended up okay, but he needed a lot of coaxing and hand-holding to jolt him out of his aversion to the reins of leadership (Judg. 6-8). Moses expressed lack of self-confidence, which debilitated him from fulfilling God's call (Ex. 4:10-17). God rebuked Moses for this kind of "humility" rather than commending him for it.

Perhaps the most poignant example of this point, however, is Saul. Given the disastrous conclusion of Saul's reign, it is easy to forget that Saul was originally God's choice for king (a choice that God eventually came to "regret," 1 Samuel 15:35). God was clear in His choice of Saul, even though Saul was reluctant to believe that he was the one deemed worthy of such an honor; he responded with meekness, self-deprecation, and timidity (1 Sam. 9:15-23). Even after he had been clearly anointed and empowered for the task, he embraced his calling with reluctance (1 Sam. 10:1-16); and, his first response to his call to kingship being made public was to literally run and hide (1 Sam. 10:22).

Are these signs of deep humility that Scripture urges God's people to acquire? No. This is something different. This is a manifestation of vanity and selfish ambition, only lacking the courage or the confidence to more overtly pursue the prestige and position privately aspired to. This is not humility; it is insecurity.

This insecurity manifests itself in many unbecoming ways. It is grounded in the same desire for recognition, the same ambition for the perks and prestige of power and position as its cousin character flaw, arrogance. In fact, displays of arrogance and conceit are often masks for insecurity.

Saul takes note of every slight, but does not have the confidence to challenge his detractors, privately or publicly (1 Sam. 10:25-27). His lack of confidence in the Lord causes him to fudge his obedience, which then must be compensated for with impetuous assertions of authority and control over areas not properly within his realm of authority. This only adds to the capriciousness of his leadership; at one moment he discards the scruples of priestly regulations and just does it himself because "people are starting to leave" (1 Sam. 13:8-13); at another moment he is ready to put his own son to death, a faithful, virtuous son who had valiantly led the king's army to a great victory in battle earlier that day (1 Sam. 14).

Every one of these problems in Saul's leadership was caused by his sense of insecurity. He was thus motivated far too much by "how is this going to make me look to my people?" This is the point of Proverbs 29:25: "The fear of man brings a snare" (forgetting the reassurance that follows, "but he who trusts in the LORD will be exalted").

A vicious cycle can also be observed: the deficiency of character that caused these failures is only made worse by the failures. Saul brooded over his misfortunes, and on the challenges and problems that continued to plague him. He was thus prone to periods of deep discouragement and depression.

Capable people around him he regarded as a threat, even those whose loyalty to him was unquestionable. Rather than being able to see them as allies he could partner with, as assets that could better enable him to accomplish the noble goals to which he and the people of God were committed, he regarded gifted people close to him as rivals, as those who made him look bad in comparison.

Insecure leaders inevitably drive away capable co-leaders. Often what results is a team of yes-men, or of work-a-day minions browbeaten, cowered, or sympathized into deference to the leader.

Saul ended up squandering the gifted team with which he had been blessed and throwing away the considerable talent and ability he had within his reach. The final years of his tenure were spent mostly on a fruitless chase of an imagined rival in a vain effort to shore up the security of his position at all costs. What a waste.

Part of the job of a leader is to project and inspire confidence and vision. When done well, genuine inspiration is generated behind a truly Spirit-led direction. When such inspiration cannot be produced authentically (and by the power of the Spirit), that is when posturing and hypocrisy typically occur.

Let's be clear: you and I are inadequate to the task of any vision that is worthwhile or divinely prompted—inadequate in our own strength and power, that is. We may be able to accomplish some things with raw talent and concentrated dedication to a task; and some leaders satisfy themselves with that medio-cre level of accomplishment. When the leader's sights are set no higher than what he or she can achieve, the vision is tame and limited; but that is also when over-confidence and arrogance can arise. Something is being accomplished, and I, I, I am the one who did it. An exaggerated accounting of what has been ac-complished, an inflated sense of what was ever envisioned, nat-urally accompanies such a misguided mentality.

At the other extreme is the person who recognizes all too well their inadequacy to the tasks before them, but who is too insecure to admit that they need help from anyone else. Yet their aspirations and ambitions remain high, so that they pres-ent themselves as a bigger deal than they are—as holier than they really are, or as the theological authority, talented entre-preneur, or managerial expert. Sometimes the only one who does not realize they are not successfully pulling off this charade is the person himself.

Genuine humility accompanied by authentic, prayerful reli-ance on God is the antidote to all of these far-too-common lead-ership cul-de-sacs and character defects. Recognition of one's limitations need not degenerate into insecurity, and recogni-tion of one's strengths and abilities need not puff one up with pride. Genuine humility allows one to recognize the *truth* about oneself in both regards.

My family and I had the privilege of attending and serving in two different churches that were pastored by two different men, both of whom struggled with a sense of inadequacy. Judging by their pulpit presence, one would never guess that they struggled with self-doubt. Their high level of giftedness in preaching and pastoral ministry disguised their secret fears of inferiority. One of them would occasionally say to the congregation in a sermon,

"I know that some of you think that I am just no good at x, or that you suspect I may have a sinful attitude in the way I go about y. I want you to know that you're wrong. It's far worse than you think."

What a disarming acknowledgement, put forth with the kind of genuine humility that enabled him as pastoral leader to carry on with the duties of his calling without apology or shame, without defensiveness or bullying. His authenticity and humility gave him space to succeed without having to cover over his failures.

This example raises the observation of an ironic truth: that the degree of pride or degree of insecurity one has may have very little to do with one's abilities or natural giftedness. Some people have tremendous levels of talent, ability, and giftedness, who yet struggle with a sense of inadequacy. Likewise there are people who have very limited levels of true ability, but who seem to genuinely believe they are God's gift to the church in their area of interest or aspiration. In the end, like so many things in life and ministry, it comes down to a matter of the heart.

Among other opportunities your seminary experience affords, you certainly have opportunity to test your heart in these matters. Every semester, at least one student in my class struggles with the idea that his or her work merited only a "B." The multitude of grades and assessments that form the warp and woof of the academic regimen provide natural incitement to either pride or insecurity.

Some people never overcome the temptation of pride and spend their lives accommodating in one way or another their fall to it. Sometimes their ministry is ruined, but not always; it is always impacted, though. They may spend their lives ministering in contexts where there is little chance that anyone will come along who is able to challenge their greatness in their own eyes. Or they may lead ministries that remain forever anemic under their headship because no one beneath them or around them is ever allowed to grow or flourish in a way that could "diminish" them, in their own eyes or in the eyes of others.

Part of the challenge to all this is that being a leader involves a certain amount of charisma, astuteness to interpersonal relationships, and skill in navigating small-group or large-group dynamics. Most ministries involve some form of public speaking. Preaching engages the minister in numerous dynamics besides exegeting the text or applying its principles to life. It involves stage presence, rhetoric, even some acting ability. The best preachers seem at least comfortable in the pulpit (even if they are not). Many preachers get a rush out of the public performance; others find it intimidating if not terrifying, week after week.

The minister-in-training should ponder carefully the kind of demeanor and overall impression he intends to set forth (rather than just assume or presume a posture). I am *not* saying that the demeanor one assumes in the pulpit should be timid, demure, or apologetic. Not in the least. The Word of God does have authority, and the communicator of God's Word should represent that authority faithfully. Also one must recognize the prophetic role of the communicator of God's Word, which is and should be corrective, confrontational, challenging, prescriptive, and directive.

Many young preachers are either reluctant to take such a role of directive authority or enjoy telling other people what to do a little too much. You should be careful about what sort of image you portray and be sure it is authentically you—a "you" that has the authority of God's Word behind you, but you.

You will likely begin developing the formation of your "pulpit style," your "stage presence," in seminary. I would hope that the seminary you attend, the homiletics professors under whom you study, will encourage you to experiment some and allow some flexibility of style that fits your personality and temperament and maturity level.

Seminary classrooms provide a temptation to posture that is similar to what the disciples experienced in the Upper Room. Rivalries for recognition as the most spiritual, the most knowledgeable, the most theologically astute, are common. "Who will be the greatest?" after graduation is a question—and an ambition—that provides no less an insidious stumbling block to seminarians than it did for the original Twelve. Posturing for approval is a snare.

So, what image are you projecting? And, what are your motives for projecting such an image? What feedback do you receive?

Confessing your own struggles is fine, so long as you fully understand your obligation to obey. Part of what is involved in the vocational calling of the minister of God's Word is the obligation to represent and convey faithfully the prophetic voice of the Spirit who speaks to His people through His Word. Mere confession of failure or weakness without repentant transformation is also a snare.

So how do you do that without phony posturing? How can you preach authentically without entering into hypocrisy or a sanctimonious spirit?

One way is to be reminded (and to remind others) that the authority of your preaching or teaching comes from God's Word, not from your own insights, abilities, or experiences. You can say and demonstrate through your actions that your conclusions from God's Word represent convictions that you must faithfully convey as part of your calling to communicate God's

Word accurately. However, you could be mistaken in your interpretation, so that, if it be shown that God's Word actually teaches something other than what you originally surmised, you will adopt that and obey that as your conviction. There is a fine line here, because there is a legitimate authority that the preacher or teacher carries as the bearer of the message of God's Word. But it is derived authority. And you are responsible to obey the *ultimate* authority every bit as much as the people to whom we are preaching or teaching.

"Beware when you think you stand, lest you fall" (1 Cor. 10:12). The heart and mind that the minister must cultivate is one that humbly realizes one's own inadequacies, who bears firmly in mind one's dependence on the Lord to be able to gain insight from God's Word and live consistently in accord with its teachings. With these realities firmly in mind, the minister should not be debilitated by them, but should *confidently* rely on the Word and boldly communicate the principles one has learned by studying His Word, aided and assisted by all the resources, tools, and training gained even by one's seminary training. This reliance on the Lord does bring with it a certain godly confidence, for He is the One who is "able to keep you from falling and to present you faultless before the presence of His glory with exceeding joy" (Jude 24).

Bold, confident reliance on the Lord by one humbly committed to serving Him forms the character of an extremely effective leader of God's people. Such a person provides a powerfully effective model for the community of faith. If that community likewise is constituted by people committed to obeying the Lord and following Him where He leads, the work of the Spirit thus enabled is such that the gates of hell cannot stand against it.

Recognize That Seminary Is an Ideological Entity

A set of sociological and historical factors should be considered when analyzing the role of the seminary in training individuals for ministry. Most seminaries were founded either by a denomination that established a school to train ministers for its churches or by exponents of a certain theological viewpoint (perceived as endangered usually) to perpetuate that theological stance. Either way, it should be recognized that seminaries are in part ideological entities, which exist in some measure to inculcate a certain viewpoint. Even if that viewpoint is neither doctrinaire nor dogmatizing, a certain ideology forms the ethos of the education. (An ideology that embraces and upholds ecumenism, for instance, is still an ideology.)

The faculty of seminaries consists of scholarly people who, after studying the Scriptures, theology, history, and the disciplines of their field for years have come to certain conclusions, who believe those conclusions are well supported by the evidence, and who can demonstrate the rationale for their conclusions deftly and persuasively. This is not necessarily a bad thing; it is just the nature of what is involved in higher education.

Now, even if you happen to be so fortunate as to have professors throughout your program who are nothing but generous to viewpoints they disagree with, who encourage nothing but fairness in the evaluation of evidence, and who are receptive to the proposal of alternative ideas and conclusions—even those proposed by their students—even then, the student is still being formed and trained, in part, to evaluate, construct, and defend arguments as part of what it means to be educated in the Scriptures, educated in theology, educated for ministry. There is nothing wrong with this as far as it goes, so long as somewhere along the way, it is acknowledged that this is what is happening and that this really is not the end of the matter.

One more role of seminary is that it "is the place where the church does its thinking," as the medieval church fathers suggested. One might even liken seminary to the research and development wing of a corporation manufacturing armaments for spiritual warfare. Think about the value of that for the soldiers on the ground. It is highly advantageous for somewhere, at some time, for some highly intelligent and knowledgeable group of people to evaluate and argue till they come to the proper conclusion as to whether aluminum, steel, copper, or some synthetic alloy is the optimal material to use for the firing pin of the rifles issued to every soldier; same thing for the helmets that protect their heads, for every part of the Humvees that transport them into battle, and so forth. There is a place for studied evaluation and argumentation with the goal of refining the final product to the strongest, best possible conclusion.

That place is well behind the lines of battle, though. It would be counterproductive for soldiers on the ground to be bickering over what is the best brand of rifle when enemy soldiers meanwhile are advancing on their position. Seminary is that place well behind the lines of battle in which the refinement of armaments, and overall philosophy of ministry (including theological orientation), strategy, and tactics is hammered out and crafted.

Ministerial students need to recognize the differences between the seminary and the church or other place of ministry "on the ground." Some believe that all ministry training should be "on the ground," on-the-job training, and that seminary training is a distraction to real ministry rather than a help.

Reservists and soldiers enlisted by conscription play a valuable role in strengthening the armed forces. Dedicated people without formal training can be highly valuable, too, in joining the fight. The valiance of people serving in the French underground in Nazi-occupied territory in World War II, for instance, is beyond question. Poorly armed, untrained, but highly adaptive, innovative, and remarkably well organized, they did much to support the overthrow of the Nazis before, during, and after the Allied invasion.

However, they probably would not have succeeded in accomplishing such an overthrow on their own. Likewise, think of how the military would be weakened were there *no* career military officers, or worse, no research-and-development segments of weapons manufacturers. One reason the Axis forces were able to move into North Africa with such ease is because they had developed fighter planes and tanks while their victims fought back with only spears and arrows. Research and development and specialized professional training are components as vital to the army of the Lord as they are to national security.

In the ministries to which we are called, the weapons of our warfare are necessary and useful; preparation and *training* for engagement in spiritual battles is essential. The potential for waste and creation of theological boondoggles is real, as well; there does need to be regular and deliberate interaction between the seminary and on-the-ground ministers lest seminary be a laboratory for creating products that no one really needs or uses. That is not the inevitable consequence, however; studied development of training and skills vital to the church and its ministries is a valuable service that a good seminary education can, should, and does provide.

Seminary students should recognize that they are on the boot-camp obstacle course, not on the actual battlefield. This training ground is the place for testing and refinement. The argumentation one engages in as a seminarian is for the development and sharpening of tools for ministry, a process different from actual use of those tools in ministry. Actual practice will look a lot different from the development process in the laboratory of the seminary. This is the difference between sharpening the ax and swinging the ax.

As a seminary student you are accumulating a knowledge base, honing a skill set, and forming an overall theological and philosophical orientation that, if done well, will serve you well in ministry for the rest of your life. However, it will only serve you so well if you recognize that when you leave seminary you are in part leaving behind the cocoon that helped form you. The point of seminary is not to take along the cocoon and re-implement its formative qualities at the place where the butterfly lands. A drill sergeant's screaming in the face of raw recruits whom he is trying to whip into shape as soldiers is not a model for military communication; nor is the conceptual argumentation engaged in among seminary students a model for pastoral communication.

Likewise the critical thinking skills and the ability to craft and sustain a solid line of argument are good tools for the development of good biblical and theological thinking. In seminary, the Bible is studied, analyzed, and dissected, its message and meaning debated and evaluated, much like a soldier being taught how to disassemble and reassemble his rifle, and how to clean it thoroughly and regularly. Yet even if quick disassembly and reassembly of the rifle impresses and delights civilian spectators, in the end that is not what the rifle is for. Likewise, that is not what the Bible—the sword of the Lord (rifle of the Lord?)—is for.

The training is not purposeless, but the training is for purposes that are beyond the training ground itself. The seminarian who uses her training in developing strong lines of argument to become argumentative is abusing her training. The seminarian who uses his knowledge of the Bible to impress people with his knowledge is as useless and misguided as the soldier who spends his entire career disassembling and reassembling his rifle for gaping crowds without ever firing a shot.

Moreover, just as some skills developed in military training are useful for the battlefield but are detrimental to assimilation into normal, civilian life, so also seminary training can have some potential liabilities. Constructing and asserting superior arguments is encouraged and affirmed in seminary, whereas collaboration with people, most of whom are less studied, less knowledgeable, and usually less concerned about tight logic, is a far more valuable skill in ministry.

Seminary graduates can often win most arguments with laypersons regarding the Bible or theology. But so what? That does not mean they are always right; even about what the biblical passage in controversy actually teaches. That is, the person with "the best argument" is not always the one who is correct. Sometimes a person may not have the knowledge or skill to put into words the insight they see (or just "sense"), but that does not mean they are wrong entirely. Likewise, a person can be wrong about the specific conclusion they are trying to draw, but they may have a point about something that forms the subtext to their thinking.

For instance, eighteenth-century medical doctors were wrong about "bad blood" being the source of disease and they did much damage to people to whom they applied leeches. Even still, they were on to something, even though their initial efforts were off. Their suppositions, though flawed, formed the baseline of discussion and experimentation that eventually developed into germ theory, which spawned a spat of medical breakthroughs that would save many lives. There is a sense in which medical practitioners at the time could have analyzed the results of "leech therapy" and (rightly) concluded that this was a wrongheaded approach to patient care. However, it would have been a serious mistake to simply dismiss, ignore, or argue against the suppositions of the theory and left it at that. The suppositions that formed even this wrong conclusion were not entirely wrong in whole and in part; the lines of logic that led to the misguided conclusion needed refinement and readjustment, not total obliteration or rejection.

It is difficult to teach collaboration and careful listening in seminary. A proper attitude can be encouraged and modeled, but the core of what is needed is a heart issue and a maturity issue.

Much academic work is independent, by its very nature. Independent thinking, independent research, and individual responsibility are all encouraged and rewarded in an academic environment. This is as it should be, as far as the academy is concerned. But one must recognize that academic skill and achievement are not the same as ministry skill or achievement; in fact in some ways the two sets of skills stand in significant contrast.

The seminary graduate who recognizes this tension between the academy and ministry stands in better shape to overcome the artificialities and superficialities of the academic training environment. For one thing, diligent work in real life ministry is rarely rewarded with tangible praise and affirmation; and often one may find oneself getting unfairly evaluated for things not your fault. No school can really prepare a student for that—other than to tell you to expect it, to be ready when it comes.

If you come out of seminary merely as the expert debater and defender of the theological positions you learned there, your seminary education was probably a waste. If you come out of seminary with a knowledge base to build on, with models of godliness embedded into your psyche of aspiration, and with facility in biblical study, problem-solving, and conflict resolution, then your investment in seminary will have been wise.

The Proper Place of the Knowledge of God

Much of what we have been considering here involves the distinction between knowing *about* God and knowing *God*. The two are not the same. Neither is particularly easy to gain, but the latter is far more difficult. Knowing God requires not only time and thought, but also relational commitment, a submissive spirit, and a predisposition to trust even when understanding is lacking.

Getting to know God as a person is highly rewarding, more desirable than gold; yea, than much fine gold—but there is a cost. Kind of like a treasure you might find in a field that requires you to sell everything you have to buy the field to get the treasure. Seminary may even be considered part of the "field," but even so it is only a means of getting to the real treasure.

I usually close the first class of my beginning course of theology by having students listen to a country song by Ty Herndon entitled, "What Mattered Most." Before I turn it on, I ask students to listen for the answer to the question, "What is this guy's problem in the song?" In the song, the man describes how he knew all the "cold facts" about his girlfriend—her hair is long, her eyes are blue, in '64, she was born in Baton Rouge, her favorite song is "In My Life," her father's tall, her mother's gone, she moved out West when she was two—but neglected to learn "what mattered most," what were her deepest heart desires and longings. Inevitably, tragically, she ends up leaving him. When the song is over, someone in the class will correctly observe, "He knew about her, but he didn't know her."

This is a great point to keep in mind about one's own relationship with one's spouse or significant other. Any relationship can grow dry over time, if "what matters most" is neglected—the passion and passionate interest in what makes the other person tick, what makes them happy, and how you can help secure that happiness, as much as it depends on you.

The same thing is true about our relationship with God. Studying the things of God is not the same as knowing God. Learning God's Word is not the same as knowing God. Preaching and teaching about God, or otherwise working for God, is not the same thing as getting to know God Himself, learning His heart, learning to enjoy what He enjoys, fostering what is most important to Him.

The next chapter discusses spiritual disciplines, which can help foster your relationship with God. Their effectiveness is spoiled, though, if you practice spiritual disciplines as a "technique" for ministry effectiveness.

Chapter 3

Disciplining Heart and Head

Pursuing Both Spiritual and Academic Disciplines
Looking for Physical Discipline

I (Paul) admire runners. Not those of us who engage in the occasional 5K race. I mean real runners, those who hit the pavement regularly. I have tried running on a daily basis, and it is difficult. It seems there is no end to the list of excuses that one can come up with when daily exercise is involved. First, there's the weather. It can be too hot or too cold. It can be raining or snowing. Most of us do not like to run even if it is too windy, but this is not a problem for "real" runners.

Other excuses are; dogs, lack of equipment, too much traffic, or no one to run with. Effective runners put aside these petty excuses and plod onward. They have learned to practice mind over matter; if they don't mind...it doesn't matter!

Committed runners run even when it is too hot or too cold, or if it is snowing or raining. They run into the wind, and they run with the wind at their back.

Question: What separates real runners from wannabes?

Answer: Real runners have *discipline*. They have trained themselves to set aside easy excuses and get on with running.

Just as a runner determines to discipline himself for the pursuit of exercise or the enjoyment of running, so believers are commanded to discipline ourselves and to lay aside the distractions of the world. The apostle Paul advised Timothy, "Discipline yourself for the purpose of godliness; for bodily discipline is only of little profit, but godliness is profitable for all things, since it holds promise for the present life and also for the life to come" (1 Tim. 4:7-8).[1]

Successfully following Jesus in your academic studies involves laying aside the weights that hinder, and learning to put on discipline as a lifestyle. As you have learned from previous chapters, you can achieve balance between learning and loving God. You do not have to put aside your devotion to Christ in order to dive deeply into an academic pursuit of who God is. The two themes of this chapter highlight learning both academic and spiritual disciplines, which, if adopted, will stand you in good stead as you embark on your journey of learning.

Only God Can Cause Growth

God is the one who brings maturity and growth into our lives.

---

1   Paul and Timothy were no doubt well aware of the schools of athletics where students rigorously trained for local and national games such as the Olympics.

We are not to strive in the energy of the flesh to become more Christlike ourselves. Paul reminded his readers in Corinth, "I planted, Apollos watered, but God was causing the growth" (1 Cor. 3:6). Since we are spiritual beings, God is working in us to conform us to His image. Paul also reminded believers in Colosse to watch out for false teachers who were "not holding fast to the head [Christ], from whom the entire body, being supplied and held together by the joints and ligaments, grows with a growth which is from God" (Col. 2:19).

The growth plan whereby Christians are rendered holy (separated for service) is a life-long process, which theologians call sanctification. This should not be confused with the moment of salvation (justification) when through faith your past, present, and future sins are forgiven based on your trust in the finished work of Christ. However, both justification (salvation) and sanctification (growth in Christ) necessarily involve faith (yielding to God). Since sanctification is God's work and not our own, His power is needed. God uses at least three change agents in our lives to produce the maturity He desires.

The first is the person and work of the *Holy Spirit*. Since God is eternal and ever-present, He is always available and at work in our lives to conform us to the image of Christ. The Holy Spirit seeks to shape and mold us toward holiness (being set apart for service).

The second agent is the *body of Christ*. God uses other believers who know you well to help bring about life change. God has instituted the church as His expression of Jesus Christ on earth at this time in history, to do His work in the world. Growth comes not in individual isolation but in interaction with fellow members of Christ's body.

A third means God uses as a tool of growth is *His Word*. The Scriptures are God's self-revelation of who He is and a record of His work in the world and throughout salvation history. These three things—the Holy Spirit, the body of Christ, and God's Word—work together to help place believers in a position where God can produce life change.

Why Use Ancient Disciplines Today?

Though God is the one who causes spiritual growth, you can put yourself in position to receive God's grace. For example, God plainly states that He, "opposes the proud, but gives grace to the humble" (Prov. 3:34; James 4:6; 1 Peter 5:5). As Dallas Willard stated in his classic work on the spiritual disciplines, "We can, through faith and grace become like Christ by practicing the types of activities he engaged in, by arranging our whole lives around the activities he himself practiced in order to remain constantly at home in the fellowship of his Father."[2] We should employ spiritual disciplines because Jesus and His earliest followers practiced them. In the early church these life disciplines placed believers in the position where they were most able to receive and act on God's grace.

Embarking on a journey of learning about God and the Bible in the context of higher education takes discipline. By practicing the spiritual disciplines you will be better prepared to face the academic rigors. By practicing spiritual disciplines alongside academic rigor you will be better able to implement the advice advocated in this volume. You can begin to learn more *about*

---

2   Dallas Willard, *The Spirit of the Disciplines* (San Francisco: Harper & Row, 1988), ix.

God and also to learn more *of* God. You can implement learning which takes place in the head *and* the heart. In this way your training can be some of the most exciting years of your life.

Think of the alternative; learning that stays in the head may remain cold and stagnant, however, learning that makes its way into the heart can become warm and inviting. If you practice learning only for learning's sake, you might quickly dry up and burn out. However, if you *practice* the truths you are being taught, you can grow in your knowledge of Christ and His ways.

Which Spiritual Disciplines?

We will first describe some of the *spiritual* disciplines that you can begin or continue to practice. Then we will define some of the *academic* disciplines that may be unique to the field of higher education. These two practices work together to point us toward godliness and Christlikeness. The Scriptures command us to "be diligent to present yourself approved to God as a work-man who does not need to be ashamed, accurately handling the word of truth" (2 Tim. 2:15). On the other hand it is not enough simply to study. We must practice what we are learning. In the Sermon on the Mount Jesus said,

> "Everyone who hears these words of mine and does them is like a wise man who built his house on rock. The rain fell, the flood came, and the winds beat against that house, but it did not collapse because it had been founded on rock. Everyone who hears these words of mine and does not do them is like a foolish man who built his house on sand. The rain fell, the flood came, and the winds beat against that

house, and it collapsed; it was utterly destroyed!"
(Matt. 7:24-27).

Practicing Spiritual Disciplines

The following is an alphabetical (though not exhaustive) listing of some of the more popular disciplines and a few words regarding their use in an academic setting. Also the practices are not magical or mystical; they are to be used as ways to train the mind, body, and spirit toward godliness. They are ways or habits that Christians down through the centuries have found useful in battling against the desires of the flesh (mortification), the pride of life (worldly lusts), and the enemy of the soul (the Devil).

Celebration

Celebration involves taking time out of normal routines to reflect on the goodness of God. This could mean celebrating a good grade on an exam or throwing a party to thank partners involved in a ministry effort. Proverbs 13:19 states, "Desire realized is sweet to the soul." Academic study can become rigorous, so take time to celebrate what God is doing in your life and in the lives of those around you.

Chastity

Today chastity has come to be known as a synonym of virginity. However, chastity involves people who are married and single. To discipline yourself toward chastity means you are thinking clear, pure thoughts regarding all areas of sexuality. The human body is made in God's image and is to be used for good works. The world, however, teaches that any sexual prohibition is a denial of a "right." Since so much of ministry involves "soul work,"

66

it is imperative that you practice the discipline of chastity both now in your preparation and later in your ministry.

Confession

Confession requires much humility. It is an opening of your private self to someone whom you trust. This can be a close friend, but normally it should involve no more than a small group of three or four. Also you may need to confess to a mentor or professor that you have fallen short in your walk with Christ. Confession keeps us from harboring secret sins in our lives and exposes the weakness of the flesh. Ultimately it is a freeing, liberating discipline that brings fresh joy and newness of life. This is more than simply a discipline. It is also a command to all Christians. As James said, "Therefore, confess your sins to one another, and pray for one another so that you may be healed. The effective prayer of a righteous man can accomplish much" (James 5:16).

"Examen"

Seminary can be an extremely busy place where academic deadlines pile up against research papers. Ignatius practiced what he called "Examen." This included five steps, which he encouraged the Jesuits to practice at noon and at the end of the day before retiring: (1) Become aware of God's presence. (2) Review the day with gratitude. (3) Pay attention to your emotions. (4) Choose one feature of the day and pray from it. (5) Look toward tomorrow. Some have called it, "Praying backward through your day."

Fasting

Going without food is probably the best known of all the spiritual disciplines. This can be done during a specific meal time, such as skipping lunch for several days. The purpose of fasting from food is to draw blood away from the stomach and into the brain so that mental acuity is heightened. The spiritual purpose is to allow the hunger pangs to remind us of our need before God. Fasting during school is possible; however, it may not be wise to fast for many days because academic life is fairly rigorous. Also a doctor should obviously be consulted if you have any medical issues such as diabetes. Also some people today are choosing to "fast" from technology. Since technology is now so pervasive I have heard students say they are fasting from television, Facebook, or Twitter by going through "digital detox."

Feasting

On occasion a good meal should be enjoyed with close friends. You are not more of a spiritual giant if you stay locked in your dorm room every day eating microwaved noodles. Feasting is not the same as gluttony. Feasting involves the joyous preparation and carefree enjoyment of a pleasurable meal and is normally accompanied by one or more friends or family members. This could take place at the end of a semester or the night before saying good-bye on a mission trip. Again, the purpose as always, is to bring glory to the Creator, and to reflect on how God brings good gifts into our lives. As Paul said, "Whether, then, you eat or drink or whatever you do, do all to the glory of God" (1 Cor. 10:31). God's people have always celebrated feast days.

Fellowship

One of the serious dangers of academic life is isolated individualism. To counter this you should set aside time for regular interaction with friends and family. It is especially important that you become involved in a local place of worship. The writer of Hebrews warned against a type of private Christianity when he counseled his readers not to forsake their "assembling together, as is the habit of some, but encouraging one another; and all the more as you see the day drawing near" (Heb. 10:25). Some students reason that since they are at seminary or studying the Scriptures on a regular basis they are simply too busy for church life. Nothing could be further from the truth. It is a terrible habit to sleep in on Sunday morning and tell friends that you worshiped with "Pastor Pillow" or "Reverend Sheets" at "Bedside Baptist."

Friendship

This discipline involves more than having a mutual acquaintance. A spiritual friend is a gift from God who takes an honest and active involvement in your life. As Solomon wrote, "Faithful are the wounds of a friend, but deceitful are the kisses of an enemy" (Prov. 27:6). You need such a friend and you need to be such a friend to another. It takes discipline to set aside regular times of authentic interaction. This is the type of friendship in which you can practice confession or encouragement. Do you have a person like this in your life?

Guidance

This discipline involves opening yourself to someone who has your best interest at heart. You need to use this discipline when making important decisions, such as where to study, what to study, what we plan on doing with our future, which person to date or marry, or even whether to rent or purchase a home. Normally guidance comes from a study of the Scriptures and advice from a few close friends or mentors. You should avoid following a fleeting feeling, doing something because we heard a song on the radio at the exact moment when we were thinking about the decision, or following the counsel of a faded billboard on a highway. It helps to talk about an important decision with three or four individuals who have godly wisdom.

Journaling

Writing down the ways in which you have seen God at work in your life is a wonderful way to add meaning to your walk with Christ. Some write out their heartfelt petitions and answers to prayers. Others record significant events, knowing they will want to review them in the future. Journaling on a consistent basis requires discipline. God commanded Isaiah, "Now go, write it on a tablet before them and inscribe it on a scroll, that it may serve in the time to come as a witness forever" (Isa. 30:8).

Lectio Divina

This spiritual discipline involves reading or listening to the words of Scripture in a deliberate way. This can be practiced alone, when you are carefully reviewing a Bible verse or other portion of Scripture, or in a group when a reader slowly emphasizes specific words, terms, phrases, or images in a passage. David Benner describes four stages in this discipline: (1) *Lectio*, prayer as attending, (2) *Meditatio*, prayer as pondering, (3) *Oratio*, prayer as responding, and (4) *Contemplatio*, prayer as contemplating.[3]

Meditation

To meditate on God or a passage of Scripture takes mental effort. This is not for the faint of heart or the easily distracted. This is

---

3   David G. Benner, *Opening to God* (Downers Grove, IL: InterVarsity Press, 2010), 53.

also a rare discipline in our frenzied society. For example, how many people do you know who deeply meditate on Christ or His teachings on a regular basis? The Psalmist called on his readers to meditate only twice a day; day and night (Ps. 1:2). You get the point: meditation should be done on a regular basis as we set our minds on things above. Christian meditation has nothing to do with non-biblical, Eastern forms of mysticism. Nowhere in the Bible are Christians called on to empty their minds. Rather "Let the words of my mouth and the meditation of my heart be acceptable in Your sight, O LORD, my rock and my Redeemer" (Ps. 19:14).

Prayer

Though countless volumes have been written on prayer, how are you incorporating this spiritual discipline into your daily walk? Is yours a prayer-less Christianity? It may help to partner with a friend or a group, or for you to attend a regularly scheduled prayer meeting. Since Jesus rose early in the morning to spend time with God the Father, how much more do we need to do this? *After* the disciples had been sent out on their ministry mission "it happened, that while Jesus was praying in a certain place, after He had finished, one of His disciples said to Him, 'Lord, teach us to pray just as John also taught his disciples'" (Luke 11:1).

Retreat

Taking time to get away from the cares of the world requires humility and planning. Most people plunge ahead in their daily lives without ever taking time for refreshment or reflection. Someone has defined "insanity" as making the same decisions over and over again and expecting different results. Choose whatever setting is most comfortable and conducive toward connecting with God: a lake house, a camp in the woods, a mountainside meadow, or a quiet countryside chapel. A retreat can last a few hours or a few days. A time of reflection can be preplanned or unscripted, but normally it involves setting aside daily responsibilities so your mind and heart can be freed to focus on Christ, His Word, and His work in the world.

Sacrifice

This discipline may require more than simply letting someone else enjoy the last slice of chocolate cake. This discipline is sometimes referred to as simplicity or frugality. Is there some area of your life where you need to cut out something? Do you really need the latest clothes, or do you already have enough? Could you provide finances for someone in need or for a project that needs additional funding? As a student, you may need to sacrifice the enjoyments that others take for granted such as hours of television viewing, weekends off, or exotic travel vacations. Jesus said, "Truly I say to you, there is no one who has left house or brothers or sisters or mother or father or children or farms, for my sake and for the gospel's sake, but that he will receive a hundred times as much now in the present age, houses and brothers and sisters and mothers and children and farms, along with persecutions; and in the age to come, eternal life" (Mark 10:29-30).

Secrecy

Did you hear about the pastor who received a medal for being the most humble person in his town, only to have it taken back by the congregation when someone saw him wearing it? When you perform a good deed, do you also feel the subtle urge to make sure everyone knows about it? Practicing anonymity requires discipline. Jesus said, "But when you give to the poor, do not let your left hand know what your right hand is doing, so that your giving will be in secret; and your Father who sees what is done in secret will reward you" (Matt. 6:3-4).

Silence

Someone has well said, "God gave us two ears and one mouth, so that we should listen twice as much as we speak." Learning to practice silence requires disciplined patience. Many people find it difficult to be alone with their thoughts for even a few moments. We surround ourselves with the din of loud music, news talk radio, the Internet, media, and all kinds of mindless noise. Must we always suffer through painful disruptions for God to get our attention? When was the last time you practiced this ancient spiritual discipline?

Simplicity

The flesh always craves more. It is a bottomless pit of unrequited wanting. Practicing this discipline, on the other hand, helps us focus on how grateful we can be for the things we possess, things that really matter. Some of us have too many books, others have closets full of clothes or garages (storage sheds) full of stuff. We cannot live an outward life fashioned around simplicity until we live this way on the inside. Academic pursuits sometimes enhance our desire for more. We feel as though we need to take one more course, hear one more lecture, receive another degree, and attend another conference and *then* we will be settled. Practicing simplicity helps strike at the heart of our living a hurried, complicated life.

Solitude

Do you feel that you always need to be around others? When you are alone for any length of time do you become bored or even slightly blue? Jesus often went alone up to the mountain-side to communicate with God the Father. Should we do any less? Practicing the discipline of solitude does not mean cutting yourself off from outside influences. Very few Christians are called to a monastic lifestyle. You need to occasionally get away from the crowds, and to resist the idea that says you must never spend a weekend alone.

Study

Yes, a season of intense study can be spiritually uplifting, and it certainly requires much discipline. We must love God with all our heart, soul, *and mind*. Peter said, "But sanctify Christ as Lord in your hearts, always being ready to make a defense to everyone who asks you to give an account for the hope that is in you, yet with gentleness and reverence" (1 Peter 3:15). In Greece the Bereans "were more noble-minded than those in Thessalonica, for they received the word with great eagerness, examining the Scriptures daily to see whether these things were so" (Acts 17:11).

Submission

Proud people have trouble with this spiritual discipline. We want to choose our own mentors, bosses, and professors. We chafe under rules and regulations we disagree with. We do not mind when we are in charge, but we grow uncomfortable when we are asked to obey. Even Jesus submitted to the will of His Father. "In the days of His flesh, He offered up both prayers and supplications with loud crying and tears to the One able to save Him from death, and He was heard because of His piety. Although He was a Son, He learned obedience from the things which He suffered" (Heb. 5:7-8). Consider an area of your life where you are struggling with submission. How do you plan to submit?

Worship

This spiritual discipline should describe all areas of the Christian life. "William Temple, renowned archbishop of Canterbury, defined worship as "quickening the conscience by the holiness of God, feeding the mind with the truth of God, purging the imagination by the beauty of God, opening the heart to the love of God, and devoting the will to the purpose of God."[4] We worship when we give glory to God who alone is worthy of our praise and adoration. Worship is not simply singing on a Sunday morning; it involves all our thoughts and actions at all times.

Academic Disciplines

In addition to the 22 spiritual disciplines mentioned above, the following 14 academic disciplines can help you achieve balance in your pursuit of head knowledge complemented with heart vitality.

Attendance

This may seem like the simplest of disciplines, but it trips up many good students. Most academic institutions take seriously the matter of class attendance. And yet some students seem to miss several classes for insignificant reasons. Why not discipline yourself to attend all classes whenever humanly possible. This one act sends a subtle message to your professor and your fellow students that you are serious about learning, and so you do not want to miss out on what God may be doing in that course. I have had students who have missed class come up to me the next class period and ask, "Did I miss anything

---

4   William Temple, cited in Roy B. Zuck, *The Speaker's Quote Book* (Grand Rapids: Kregel, 2009), 555.

important?" This does not leave a good impression. In addition, skipping class or checking a box in an on-line course to say you have listened or watched a course when you have not done so mitigates against your goal of becoming an authentic minister.

Eating right

Seminary is notorious as a place where poor eating habits are developed. Late-night pizza parties and a regular breakfast diet of coffee and doughnuts do not help build mental and physical stamina. Drinking energy drinks loaded with high levels of sugar and caffeine in an attempt to fuel all-night study sessions is not wise. You may feel a spike in energy at 2a.m. as you try to finish a research paper but you will no doubt feel groggy in an early morning class. Follow the apostle Paul's advice for "temple upkeep." He urged the Corinthians, "Or do you not know that your body is a temple of the Holy Spirit who is in you, whom you have from God, and that you are not your own?" (1 Cor. 6:19).

Exercise

Most of us probably feel like we could use more exercise. And yet how many of us act on our gnawing conviction? It is difficult to be a student and also attempt to live a healthy lifestyle. Most of your time is spent sitting. You sit in class, in the library, in chapel, in worship, when you are reading, and when you are writing papers. You will need to discipline yourself to find a form of exercise you enjoy. This is helpful to your mind, body, and soul. Being a whole person involves growth in knowledge, character, and physical fitness.[5]

---

5   Believing that the spiritual, and not the physical, is what matters to God is a pagan notion. Dallas Willard says, "The spiritual and the bodily are

Citation

If you have not already done so, you need to get in the habit of citing your work. Almost everything you write will be a reflection of another person's work, so you will need to cite by footnotes or endnotes where you found the ideas you are quoting. Without proper citation, you are passing off as your own the ideas of another. So when in doubt, cite. Also, you may want to begin a method for storing or collecting some of the citations you believe you may use on a regular basis. During a three- or four-year course of study you will write many papers and may even write a thesis or dissertation. It is frustrating to try to locate something you have read and cannot locate. Much of this was formerly done on paper but now software programs abound that can help you manage quotations, citations, and references.

Comparison

One of the worst mistakes young seminarians make is comparing themselves to someone else in a class, dorm, or degree program. God created you with your own unique set of gifts and talents. It is a disservice to yourself and others to constantly ask, "What did you receive on the exam?" Or, "What did the professor say about your paper?" If you are studying to learn more about God, why not leave the results up to Him? The sin of comparison can either inflate or depress your sense of self-worth. One day you may feel as though you are a better preacher, teacher, or counselor than another person, but the next day you may believe you will never be able to preach, teach, sing, raise funds, write, or research like the person who sits next to

---

by no means opposed in human life—they are complementary" (*The Spirit of the Disciplines*, 75).

you in chapel. Avoid comparing yourself with other students. Paul wrote, "Now there are varieties of gifts, but the same Spirit. And there are varieties of ministries, and the same Lord. There are varieties of effects, but the same God who works all things in all persons" (1 Cor. 12:4-6).

GPA

Grade Point Average is a delicate issue. On the one hand you should not worry about the grades you are getting so long as you are doing your best work and giving your best effort (working for an audience of One). On the other hand, if you sense you are really enjoying the academic life and are feeling called to further study, your GPA could become an important measure of how you are doing if you are planning on additional training. Some schools admit only students with a specific grade point average. But regardless of your future goals or plans, you are not the sum of your GPA! All professors have had students in their office at the end of a semester asking (begging!) for a .01 percent increase in their grade which they felt they deserved or needed. Your GPA does not equate to your salvation or sanctification. A lower GPA will not make God love you less, and a higher GPA will not make God love you more.

Limited knowledge

Many young seminarians are surprised to discover that they cannot learn all there is to know about the Bible, God, Jesus Christ. As with other academic disciplines, the more you learn, the more you have yet to learn. While it is important to study to show ourselves strong in the Scriptures and the things of God, it is important to remember that as finite humans we can never fully comprehend the mind or ways of God. Solomon said,

"But beyond this, my son, be warned: the writing of many books is endless, and excessive devotion to books is wearying to the body" (Eccl. 12:12). There are mysteries about God that we will never fully comprehend. God is infinite; we are not. "For My thoughts are not your thoughts, nor are your ways my ways, declares the LORD. For as the heavens are higher than the earth, so are my ways higher than your ways and my thoughts than your thoughts" (Isa. 55:8-9).

Openness

One of the difficulties of beginning a new course of study is working at staying open and flexible to new ideas. You may have been raised in a certain tradition or denomination. However, all human institutions are flawed. There is truth in other styles of worship and forms of relating to God. It is helpful to learn from others whom God brings into your life. You may be surprised and refreshed with how a new discipline or worship activity brings you closer to God. Obviously this does not mean you should abandon what you deeply believe. But, you can hold your beliefs at arm's length as you read more widely than you have before and open yourself to new works of God in the world. Do not let your approach to God become stale or routine. Jesus said, "And when you are praying do not use meaningless repetition as the Gentiles do, for they suppose that they will be heard for their many words" (Matt. 6:7). Remember that good and godly people can disagree on a topic and still be brothers and sisters in Christ.

Plagiarism

You must not pass off as your own the thoughts and ideas of others. Today pastors and ministry workers are cutting and pasting ideas and thoughts from the Internet without giving proper credit to the source(s). Others are downloading entire sermons or homilies and presenting them as their own work. Recently a student told me that he had heard the same sermon at two different church services. The only difference was that some of the place names in the illustrations differed. When in doubt always go to great lengths to show that you are citing or relaying the ideas, thoughts, or words from someone else when they are not your own. If you are involved in a group project, you may also be asked to show which part of the assignment you were involved in and which parts you were not. Avoiding plagiarism can be an academic *and* spiritual discipline in your life.

Prayer
Seasoned academicians encourage students to pray before, during, and after each class. Why not pray as you are writing a paper or taking an exam? Someone has well said, "As long as there are exams there will be prayer in schools!" At seminary your prayer life may become virtually non-existent. How could this happen? Sometimes when you are involved in the study of Scripture and with godly people, then prayer can fall through the cracks. We become too busy to pray. Obviously prayer is both a spiritual and an academic discipline. However, it is unique in that prayer helps us understand what we are studying as God grants illumination to our thoughts and understanding. For example, pray over your language studies, asking God not only to help you receive good grades on exams, but also that your understanding of the Scriptures will enable you to preach His Word more effectively.

Research
Pursuits in higher education often involve the difficult academic discipline of research. This involves searching for what other

gifted thinkers have written on a particular topic. It may also involve using statistical analysis or first-person interviews. Academic research can be exciting and invigorating, but it can also be difficult, grueling work. In the midst of the "fog" of research you can begin to lose the vision of why you enrolled in seminary in the first place. During the first couple of weeks of school, everything may seem fresh and new. Many have described it as making leaps in their spiritual life, or like attending the best Bible study ever. However, after mid-term exams, Christmas, or spring break, a more clarified realization settles in, and academic research is difficult! It is important to keep your long-term goals in mind and to say with the psalmist, "For you, O LORD, have made me glad by what You have done, I will sing for joy at the works of Your hands" (Ps. 92:4). Academic "suffering" lasts only for a night, but joy comes in the morning.

Respect

Young students may easily lose respect for older traditions and even aging professors. However, God calls us to honor those who have gone before us. The apostle Paul urged the Roman Christians, "Render to all what is due them: tax to whom tax is due; custom to whom custom; fear to whom fear; honor to whom honor" (Rom. 13:7). No one is advocating poor academic work. However, it does no good to denigrate the service of a mentor or professor who may not be the flashiest or most popular on campus. Know that God is using a variety of sources to pour into your life. He is preparing you for the service you will be undertaking on His behalf and in His strength. Avoid gossiping about faculty, staff, or fellow students. Show deep, authentic respect to all who are journeying with you in your pursuit of the things of God.

Rest

Like eating and exercise, you also need proper rest for your mind and body. Of course there may be nights where you are "up at all hours" studying or preparing for an academic deadline. However, some wrongly allow this to become a lifestyle rather than an occasional occurrence. The psalmist wrote, "It is vain for you to rise up early, to retire late; to eat the bread of painful labors; for He gives to His beloved even in his sleep" (Ps. 127:2).

Study

This may be the academic discipline you are most involved in during your time in seminary. You will need to discipline yourself to have adequate time for reading and reflection. If you find that you are spending all your time working at a job, neglecting friends and family, and still not studying, you are cheating yourself of your opportunity to learn and grow. Placing a book under your pillow will not enable you to learn what is in the book. Learning requires work. You may want to enlist a "study buddy" or a small study group to hold yourself accountable. Do not get mad at God if you receive a poor grade on an exam or paper when you took little time for study. God has endowed you with a healthy mind, so use it for His glory to the best of your ability.

Review these spiritual and academic disciplines. Think through the ones you believe you will struggle with the most and which ones you feel will not be as much of a challenge. Formulate a strategy on how you plan to implement these disciplines in your life. Some may be emphasized more than others during specific seasons of your study, but all of them are important for growth in Christlikeness.

Disciplining Heart and Head

The goal is to have a healthy relationship between the head and the heart, the academic and the spiritual, to grow and mature as a whole person and a believer. Often when our entire focus is driven by the pursuit of academics and the accumulation of knowledge we can become spiritually cold. Avoiding this disaster is the topic of the next chapter.

Chapter 4

AVOIDING SPIRITUAL FROSTBITE

Having a Vital Relationship with God While Pursuing Excellence in Academic Study

"It's a good life, if you don't weaken."

That statement has now become both a song and a book, both on a very different subject than our focus here. Yet, it is an apt description of the Christian life—especially a life committed to Christian ministry.

Some people pursue vocational ministry in the hope that doing so will kick-start their relationship with God, or will revitalize their spiritual life. This is a noble thought, but it is tragically misguided. It is like someone taking up mountain climbing as a way of getting some exercise.

The truth is that life in ministry is a challenge to those already fit. The threat of frostbite increases as one scales the mountain, hampering even those in admirable condition. Frostbite can be lethal if untended.

This chapter explores the challenges to spiritual vitality

faced by those in ministry, particularly those taking up specialized academic study of biblical and theological matters in preparation or as part of one's livelihood. Paradoxically, devotion to the study of spiritual matters can serve as a drain on one's spiritual life.

Spirituality Fatigue, Or Making the Profound Routine

Few people outside of my family know this about me, but I (Todd) started out in college as a music major. I suppose I never will know whether I had the talent to actually make a living as a musician, but in high school I had some music training, had done some performing, enjoyed the thrill of being in front of an audience, and all this had congealed into a real passion for music. When I got a scholarship to college to pursue it, I was sure this was the leading of the Lord.

However, something happened when I took up music as a vocational pursuit. I had never minded practicing before, but in college, music majors were required to practice between 10 and 20 hours each week. No longer did people listen to my performances for enjoyment of a "talented-for-a-high-school-kid's" display of art; now my performances were scrutinized and critiqued by people far more talented than I. These people listened carefully for the *flaws* they could detect in my performance. Over time, I found myself despising what I had once loved.

What is more, I found out it was not just me. I remember one year practicing for weeks with a choir, orchestra, and professional soloists to give a grand Christmas concert. One of the soloists was my music teacher. One day in class she disclosed to her music students, "After the concert, there will be no music of any kind heard at my house for the duration of the Christmas break!" We all laughed (she did not), but she was serious; and in fact we not only knew she was serious, we understood. "Familiarity breeds contempt" is an aphorism we all knew to be true.

I eventually dropped my major in music to a minor, and regained my enjoyment of music (as a hobby).

Similar drawbacks and negative dynamics accompany whatever one pursues as one's vocation. "Do what you love; love what you do" is good career counseling. Still, a phrase my wife has taught me is also true: "There is a reason they call it work."

Every Christian is encouraged to cultivate healthy habits of Christian living. This is hard enough to keep up when one is just a "regular Christian." What happens when your Christian walk is your vocation, when your "work" is also your ministry for the Lord?

Some realism is appropriate in this. Your knowledge of the Bible is a "trade" that is needed (and in a way is being paid for) by the people of God. Once you enter the ministry as your vocational call, you are no longer in it for just "you." Your Bible study, your prayer life, your walk with God—all these important aspects of your life, are no longer just for your personal benefit; people are counting on you to keep healthy and skilled in all these things.

Christian leaders need to recognize the challenge to the soul and the temptations that come along with routine activities. They must recognize that regarding the profound as mundane, the extraordinary as all too ordinary, is a common occupational hazard. Each seminary student and Christian leader needs to recognize that they are not alone in experiencing this melancholy experience in their vocation.

At times, you may not feel like praying. But you should get out your prayer list and pray anyway. At times, you will not feel like preaching or teaching, much less preparing for your delivery; and then you need to prepare to deliver the next one just seven days later.

A teacher has a different, but very similar challenge. Thinking through the details of a course and preparing the lesson plans can be both challenging and fun, but the shine of it can wear off by the third or fourth time one teaches it. Students' faces change, but it can feel like the same hands go up, the same questions raised. It can be hard to keep one's passion for the subject. And then there is the psychological phenomenon of being "the only teacher you hear" so regularly; it is natural to become more and more convinced of what you are saying—such that alternative viewpoints become harder to hear fairly. Patience with rival theories can wear thin. That is the land where crotchety professors come from.

Freshness and passion are vital ingredients to a vibrant ministry and also to a vibrant walk with God. Duty and repetition are natural enemies of freshness and passion. But every person in ministry must get up and deliver their message or lesson anyway because that is the job.

Burn-out may occur, when the routine, accompanied with stress and disappointment, moves from boredom to resentment to bitterness (or just a simple inability to "do it even one more time"). So you should try to avoid moving from experiencing normal dry spells and frustration to a prolonged period of spiritual or personal ill health.

My wife, Linda, and I have been happily married for over 25 years. We have a good marriage, but that does not mean that every minute of every day of those 25 years has been exuberant or passionate. There are dry spells; there are periods in which our passionate commitment to life together involves passionate disagreement, expressed in animated "discussion"! We recognize that for our relationship to be healthy and vibrant the whole relationship cannot be allowed to languish in lifeless boredom, nor to tolerate extended periods of seething anger. Part of our commitment to each other involves making sure that we "keep our accounts short," keeping our romance alive by special outings, and spending time alone with just each other sometimes in an extended, romantic weekend getaway (for example on our anniversary weekend).

However, *most* of our lives together is lived in the simple, mundane, day-to-day activities that in themselves represent no grand achievement, no fireworks, and little passionate excitement. Our love is expressed through a pot of coffee here, a snuggle in front of the TV there; a "don't worry, I'll pick him up from soccer practice this time," or a "you've had a busy day; I'll go through the drive-through so you don't have to cook tonight."

A minister's life with God works in much the same way. Much of it can feel like a daily grind of rituals, message preparation, visitation, and other ministerial activities; or, for a teacher, tweaking the syllabus goals for the umpteenth time, reading yet another book, grading yet another stack of papers. None of it may seem like much. Yet the truth is that we are engaged in significant Kingdom work, despite what may seem like bland ordinariness. The grand work of God that He is doing in and through you will likely be seen only over the long haul.

Occasional, passionate "revivals" may occur in either you or the people to whom you are ministering, or both. However, much of the work of the Spirit in your midst will likely be more subtle, in incremental steps gradually producing fruit over time.

This "is like a man who casts the seed upon the soil, goes to bed at night and gets up by day" and discovers that the seed has sprouted up and grown—how, exactly, he does not know. "The soil produces crops by itself; first the blade, then the head, then the mature grain in the head" (Mark 4:26-28). Somehow, one day you look behind you and a field of corn has arisen where just yesterday, it seems, you were doing nothing but furrowing row after row of dirt.

Disillusionment

> *"Behold, I lay in Zion a choice stone,*
> *a stumbling stone, a stone to strike,*
> *a costly cornerstone to serve as the foundation stone.*
> *And he who believes in Him will not be disappointed."*

Three times in the New Testament, some form of this merger of Isaiah 8:14 and 28:16 is quoted (see Rom. 9:33; 10:11; and 1 Peter 2:6-8). The combination of the two passages from Isaiah presents a paradoxical point: the stone is strong; it will hold up the whole building God intends to construct. The one who trusts in that stone will not be disappointed. Yet on the other hand the stone does not look like much. It has the appearance of frailty or of plain ordinariness; it does not look like the kind of special stone one would choose as a cornerstone for the foundation.

From here the imageries coalesce together to form almost a narrative. The people who reject the stone and cast it aside throw it into their walking path where they continually trip over it. Thus the stone holds a dual potential. It will either support a castle worthy of occupation by God Himself, or it will serve as an obstacle that people stumble over, sending them headlong as they fall flat on their face, where it then rolls on the one who rejected it.

So the one who relies on the stone will not be disappointed. In two of the three times in the New Testament that these Isaiah verses are cited the focus is *not* on these positive implications for the one who trusts in the stone, but on the dire consequences confronted by those who stumble over the deceptively ordinary-looking cornerstone.

Those who trust in the stone are not disappointed, but those who invest their lives trying to get people to trust in the stone, only to see them reject it and insist on tripping over it again and again, may find themselves often disappointed. This disappointment is part of the burden borne by the conscientious minister of the gospel.

This is one place where the seminary environment is a mixed blessing. It provides a nurturing context that is refreshing and exhilarating, but it can also set up the young idealist for disillusionment.

A good seminary provides regular contact with successful ministry models that inspire the imagination, and encourage the student to consider cutting-edge ministry ideas that embolden innovation for the Lord's work. The real-life world, though, usually greets the person with a more challenging context than they anticipated. Often it is difficult to spark enthusiasm, or sometimes even to garner cooperation of co-laborers. As the imagination gives way to reality, as idealism gives way to the mundane, discouragement can result.

Dreaming big, particularly if those dreams are prompted by the Holy Spirit, can be a good thing. Wishing for a significant role in God's Kingdom purposes is not wrong; the one who aspires to be an elder/pastor "desires a noble task" (1 Tim. 3:1 NIV).

Chapter 4

Even when one's aspirations are large and noble, much of the Christian life and much of Christian ministry consists of nothing grander than putting one foot in front of the other in one's walk with God. Much character is built and much vision achieved through consistent practice of restraint, accompanied by the practice of disciplines. This can result in a disciplined Christian life that inspires others to do the same. No greater calling, no nobler aspiration, no better investment of one's life can exceed that of working for the Lord.

However, in the day to day and the here and now, it often does not feel so grand and great. Getting a seminary education or working in a church-related ministry may not always feel so great. Jonah ran from God's plan, not because he did not understand it but because he *did* understand it and did not like it. Moses, Joshua, and Elijah served as top spokesmen for God, but each of them had moments of questioning not only his own role, but also whether God's plans were correct.

David was a man after God's own heart, who walked with God and "did what was right in the sight of the LORD, and had not turned aside from anything that He commanded him all the days of his life, except in the case of Uriah the Hittite" (1 Kings 15:5). Yet even he was royally irked at God for what seemed like divine pettiness when God snuffed out the life of his worker, Uzzah, for the "crime" of trying to save the ark of the covenant from falling to the ground (2 Sam. 6:6-11). Most preachers who preach through that incident find themselves explaining what God did and why He did it, but they can also find it easy to relate to David's "anger against the Lord" at the time.

This is part of what it means to have a real relationship with God once the "full commitment to Him" part is settled. It is not unlike the dynamics of living with your spouse. Every elderly married couple knows when they observe wedding ceremonies at which the young couple professes their eternal love for each other, "Now, the real test of their love begins."

Now that you have chosen each other as the one to whom you are solely committed for life, can you live together happily? Can you share a bathroom? Can you share a checkbook? What happens when he likes his bacon crisp, but she likes her bacon flimsy, and all the thousands upon thousands of other details that no one ever could possibly think about before they were married?

The dynamics of entering vocational ministry are similar. Once you have been welcomed in a ministry and the "ministry honeymoon" is over, how will you respond to people's problems, gripes, pettiness, and expectations?

Beyond the difficulty of the work, though, what about when God does not seem to fulfill your expectations? How will you respond when you have prayed for healing for someone in your congregation, but God does not respond? You can vent your frustrations to God, but you may wonder if He is listening. Knowing that God has the power to solve various problems and yet does not do so may well increase your frustration. You may tend to think, "God, with all your power, why can't you solve this little problem?"

Many people who have seriously committed themselves to God struggle at times with discouragement and disillusionment. Knowing that God's power, might, wisdom, and love are so great, and yet experiencing problems and obstacles to good and worthy goals makes for disillusionment. This is especially disconcerting when most of our problems are relatively small and could be easily overcome if God would just do so. But He often does not.

The power of discouragement increases with the level of frustration and injustice, especially when the wicked seem to prosper and the righteous suffer: "O LORD, how long?!" is a question Bible characters often asked (cf. Pss. 13, 74, 94, and Hab. 1:2). The moans and cries to God from His faithful but frustrated followers arise not just from Scripture, but from the gospel songs, spirituals, hymns, and worship songs from God's people through the ages. "Farther along, we'll understand it." "We'll talk it over in the by and by." "I'll ask the reasons; He'll tell me why." "Does Jesus care?" "On the road marked with suffering, blessed be the name."

The truth is: there are easier bosses. Human bosses have some obligation to explain company policy to employees and must in theory be open to explaining how this or that decision is consistent with company policy; God is under no such obligation. Human bosses are committed to forwarding the goals of the organization, with objectives for "employee development" listed only to the extent that affect the employee's job performance; God restrains Himself to no such limitations. Here we touch upon what is probably the heart of the matter.

The goals God has in mind are not just the goals of career success or organizational expansion. Organizational success may be primary in our minds, but that may not be much of a priority for God. He is most interested in character development, heart development, faith development. Little of this has to do with skill development, planning strategy, or talent, except insofar as these things touch on elements of integrity, character, virtue, or commitment to Him. When we forget this, we become prime targets for disillusionment.

A question to ask yourself as you undergo your seminary training is this: Can you work for God as your "boss"? Does your commitment to the ministry reflect your commitment to obeying God, no matter what? Can you say, with Job, "Though he slay me, yet will I hope in Him" (Job 13:15 NIV)?

This is what Jesus meant when He said, "Count the cost"

(Luke 14:25-33). To those who seek the rewards of the Kingdom, He asks, in essence, "but can you really bear the cost?"
(Mark 10:35-38). Keeping in mind that "it is better that you
should not make a vow to God than that you should vow and not
pay" (Eccl. 5:5), you should be very careful in what commitment
you make to God regarding your entering the ministry. Can you
really work for God as your "boss"—not just as general master
of your life, Lord and King of the universe overall—but as "chief
executive officer" of your church or organization (in which the
goals are purposely aligned with goals of the Kingdom that may
be largely intangible and immeasurable, humanly speaking)?

There are many friends who can work together, but have
the relationship strained if one becomes boss over the other.
Many husbands and wives love one another and work fine together building a home, but have trouble should they try to go
into business together. You may love God wholeheartedly; you
may be committed to obeying Him with your life; you may know
Him fully as your Lord and Savior. That still does not answer
the question, "Can you work for Him as your 'boss'?"

Some seminary students seem to aspire to the ministry as
their vocation because they really want "to work for themselves,"
"to be their own boss," only with the mantle of Divine approval and the rewards of Christian service besides. This mentality
destines the person for a fall, probably from pride and possibly
from disillusionment.

The Relationship between Critical Thinking and a Critical Spirit

Quality academic training of any kind encourages critical
thinking, the ability to test hypotheses, evaluate arguments

for their validity, to assess data, and to determine whether data used to support a case is sufficient to bear the weight of argument assigned to it. These are disciplines of the mind needed for sorting truth from error, which is something highly valued in a leader.

The book of Proverbs was written to help hone just such leadership skills of young leaders of Israel. The book focuses on character development (involving development of the leader's heart to be committed to truth and justice), the ability to discern truth, to assess cases, and to come to wise decisions.

Besides the warnings against more obvious temptations to compromise the truth, like colluding with those who "wink the eyes" and "point the feet" in scam operations (Prov. 6:13; 16:30), the book also includes adages such as Proverbs 14:4, "Where no oxen are, the manger is clean; but much increase comes by the strength of the ox." The point seems to be: Some things have an obvious downside to them, which may even be more obvious at first (having an ox means shoveling up a lot of manure!) but do not base your evaluation on the drawbacks alone. In the end, having an ox is worth it, given the increase in production it provides. One may recast Proverbs 14:4 in modern parlance as follows: "Where there is no seminary education, one has to write no papers; but much benefit stems from having a seminary education."

Sharp reasoning skill is encouraged and honed by Scripture itself. Yet sharp thinking is no substitute for depth of character. The two are not equal in value; it is better to be a person submissive of spirit and soft of heart to the Lord's will than simply smart. Solomon himself ended up finding this out the hard way.

Nor are the two mutually exclusive. In fact a person of character who also has discernment, including incisive, keen reasoning ability, is a person of ideal leadership quality. This is the ideal that Scripture advocates in both the Old Testament—especially Proverbs—and the New Testament—especially in passages that list qualifications for elders/pastors.

Cultivating analytical skills brings with it the possibility of some liabilities. As one's reasoning and analytical ability improves, as the person becomes more discerning and wise, it is easy for the person to become "wise in their own eyes."

Can you see how that happens? As you develop skills of reasoning, you grow accustomed to being right. As you cultivate the ability to persuade, using sound logic and articulate rhetoric, you grow accustomed to being respected as one who speaks with authority. Eventually, you grow accustomed to having your views accepted, adopted, and implemented.

Frankly, this could put you in a dangerous frame of mind. Several Bible passages address this issue.

> "Trust in the LORD with all your heart, and do not lean on your own understanding. In all your ways acknowledge Him, and He will make your paths straight. Do not be wise in your own eyes; fear the Lord and turn away from evil" (Prov. 3:5-7).

> "The way of a fool is right in his own eyes, but a wise man is he who listens to counsel" (Prov. 12:15).

> "Woe to those who call evil good, and good evil; who substitute darkness for light and light for darkness; who substitute bitter for sweet, and sweet for bitter! Woe to those who are wise in their own eyes, and clever in their own sight!" (Isa. 5:20-21).

"Be of the same mind toward one another; do not be haughty in mind, but associate with the lowly. Do not be wise in your own estimation" (Rom. 12:16)

Perhaps most straightforward of all, given Proverbs' well-known descriptions of the foibles of the fool, is Proverbs 26:12: "Do you see a man wise in his own eyes? There is more hope for a fool than for him."

The challenge of accompanying any academic study with the reminder not to become puffed up, not to become wise in one's own eyes, applies no less to the academic study of Scripture, theology, church history, and Christian education than to other fields of academic study. In fact, the need for this reminder in pastoral service may be even more pronounced. A microbiologist who is wise in her own eyes may be a pain in the neck to work with, but may do little harm beyond annoyance to those who work alongside her in the laboratory. But a minister who is wise in his own eyes can do damage to the well-being of an entire church body, or to the spiritual well-being of generations of believers who sit under his ministry.

Being wise in one's own eyes makes a person obnoxious, narrow, intolerant, boorish, argumentative, and impatient with those around him, but numb to his own true condition. Conversations seem to degenerate into adversarial competitions to demonstrate the correctness of one's viewpoint. Eventually people may well give up trying to offer suggestions and counsel to the person who considers himself wise.

This phenomenon is well known in the halls of academe. The ditty originally said of Harvard University students could well be said of many seminary students as well:

You can always tell a Sophomore,
he's so sedately gowned.
You can always tell a Junior,
By the way he struts around.
You can always tell a Freshman,
By his timid looks and such.
You can always tell a Senior,
but you cannot tell him much.
—Source unknown

With the increase of knowledge and mastery of any subject comes naturally an increase in confidence and a sense of authority.

Seminary is supposed to be a place that cultivates leadership potential, and that hones leadership skills in leading organizations in vision, call, and direction. Likewise seminary is supposed to increase one's knowledge of and facility with the Scriptures, so that the seminary graduate can speak with some authority on what the Bible teaches, and how its message should be applied to specific contexts.

However, there is a vast gulf between carrying out the authority of one's ministerial office and being authoritarian, between speaking with appropriate confidence what Scripture teaches and being wise in one's own estimation, and between using one's knowledge and skill for advancing a vision for the organization and using one's knowledge and skill simply to get one's own way. The vast gulf that should exist between proper pastoral nurturing and narcissistic power-grabbing is preserved by what actually may be a fine line in one's heart.

When the Bible speaks of humility, it does not mean thinking of yourself as stupid, but rather using your knowledge and reasoning to forward what is best for others rather than simply looking out for your own interests. The life trajectory is set in the heart but manifested in the life lived.

"Humility of mind" is appropriate for leaders, not just as a "technique" for getting ideas through, but because the perspective of the leader is limited, and sometimes flawed. Proverbs' repeated directive to seek counsel (Prov. 1:5; 11:14; 12:15; 15:22; 24:6) is not just a means to manipulate people into taking ownership of decisions that the leader had made. Rather, counsel is needed in order to add others' perspective to one's own, to add others' knowledge base and experience to one's own. Counsel from others helps get better ideas to the surface, ideas that can result in better decision-making.

"Humility of mind" is appropriate in the academic realm, too. Increased mastery of any field should have a humbling effect, as the student comes to recognize how much there is to learn, how much he or she does not know, and the impossibility of coming to know all that could be known in any given field even if one devotes one's lifetime to studying it.

At the annual meeting of the Society of Biblical Literature, biblical and theological scholars gather from all over the world to hear the latest ideas in cutting-edge scholarship, to propose their carefully studied hypotheses in their particular areas of specialty and to receive feedback and critique, and to trade ideas and perspectives with the most knowledgeable scholars in the world. Every year, early on the Sunday morning of the meeting week, this august group of scholars gathers for a worship service, including hymn singing, participation in liturgy, and a homily. I have often thought that there could hardly be a more intimidating group to which one could be called upon to deliver a homily. In November of 2010, Dr. Karen Jobes began her homily that morning with this disarming observation, a saying she had picked up somewhere along the way in her academic pilgrimage:

> When someone studies enough that they think they know everything, they are awarded a Bachelor's degree. When one comes to recognize that they may not know everything, they are awarded a Master's degree. And, when they realize that no one else knows either, they are awarded a Ph.D.!

Unfortunately, some scholars readily give the impression of knowing it all and of being arrogant. However, the *best* scholars are characterized by humility, despite their vast knowledge. True scholars are lifelong learners, who enjoy meeting and talking with people more knowledgeable than they, rather than being *intimidated* by people more knowledgeable than they. And by the way, there is always someone more knowledgeable than oneself. A true scholar is fascinated and humbled by how much he or she still has to learn. How different from the poseur who waxes eloquent as an expert and with his authoritative ideas. In the land of the blind, the one-eyed man is king!

Much of what we are raising here concerns the heart-motive for one's learning. A seminarian's study of the Scriptures, theology, and history can be put to valuable service for the people of God or it can be put to the service of a self-fascinated tyrant's takeover of some ministry empire.

After teaching the segment on logic and rhetoric to seminary students, I will tell them that they should now use what they have learned not just to win arguments, and not just to spot fallacies of reasoning in their own or others' arguments. Instead they should use their knowledge of proper reasoning to help other people frame the best case for their viewpoints—even when they may *disagree* with the case the other party is trying to make. That is using wisdom, knowledge, reasoning, and logic to *help* others rather than to promote oneself.

In ministry the best role a leader can take in a controversial discussion is often that of referee or mediator, rather than as one of the contenders in the fight. There are times when you will view a point or decision so crucial that contending for your view on the matter is necessary, but those times should actually be few. On most points of contention, even if your side "wins," the costs of alienation and adversarial relations make the gains of "winning" hardly worth it.

On the other hand, if the minister can use his or her knowledge and abilities to strengthen the voice of others, then that knowledge, ability, and skill can be a source of service, rather than a source of power or domination. A minister who gains the reputation of being one who is quick to listen, and slow to speak, of being a leader whose clear intention is to secure what is best for everyone—not just get his or her own way, and is known for being one who sees first the strength of another person's viewpoint rather than the weaknesses, will find it easier to persuade people of viewpoints he or she considers crucially important.

A diplomat who had met separately with two world leaders in the late 1930s later reported, "When I was with the first, I felt like I was talking to the smartest man in the world; when I was with the second, however, he made me feel like *I* was the smartest man in the world!" He was being genuinely complimentary to both, but the greater compliment was to the latter.

These are not just "leadership techniques." Nor are these merely ways of "winning people over" to one's own side, or of "picking one's battles" so as to get one's way when a person really wants to get some plan or idea accepted. A spiritual dynamic underlies the points in view here.

James wrote about there being two kinds of "wisdom." The very fact that the "wrong kind" of wisdom still masquerades as "wisdom" suggests that the detrimental kind of rationality still can appear to be "wise," knowledgeable, smart, articulate. Both kinds of "wisdom" can sound persuasive; both kinds of wisdom may use incisive, logical argumentation. This is exactly why James suggested that discernment is necessary to distinguish between the two.

What are the diagnostic tests by which one can tell which is which? According to James the difference can be spotted by discerning (1) the general characteristics of the "wisdom" forwarded; (2) the motive with which the point is forwarded; and (3) the dynamic in the community that results from the "wisdom" submitted. James 3:13-18 discusses these two kinds of "wisdom"—wisdom "from above" and wisdom that is "natural, earthly, demonic."

Wisdom from Above	Wisdom That Is Natural, Earthly, Demonic
General Characteristics: Gentleness Good behavior Pure Peaceable ("peace-seeking") Reasonable Guileless ("without hypocrisy")	**General Characteristics:** Bitterness Arrogance Disingenuousness

Wisdom from Above	Wisdom That Is Natural, Earthly, Demonic
Motive: Righteousness Peace	**Motive:** Jealousy Selfish ambition
Result: Mercy Peace and harmony Good fruits	**Result:** Disorder Strife (contentious disagreements) Every evil thing

Think about some congregational meeting, elders' meeting, faculty meeting or student council meeting where you have witnessed some controversy erupt into heated argument. The above chart, applied as a diagnostic test, can help sort out "wisdom from above" from "wisdom from below." Even though there is such a thing as a well-meaning argument that is just wrongheaded, and even though sometimes it is difficult to tell what exactly is motivating a person to forward a certain line of argument, the above layout from James 3 is remarkably effective at helping godly leaders at least know what to look for, and what questions to pursue to find out what is *really* the issue. And if something sounds like a good idea, but for some reason it is causing nothing but strife and contention in the ranks of otherwise good, dependable congregants or members of the team, one had best beware.

Critical thinking is a scholarly quality that is both taught and encouraged in seminary. Independent thinking is encouraged in the academic environment. This is well and good, but it is for mature audiences only. A person who is in ministry but who has not matured spiritually may find that these skills of critical thinking can sour into something that becomes an instrument of the devil.

A critical spirit makes for an unpleasant colleague and a despotic leader. Know-it-alls are not just irritating; they make bad decisions, because they can never take into account a sufficient number of considerations, variables, or likely consequences of their decisions, for they draw on their own limited, flawed knowledge and perspective.

God has designed the body of Christ in such a way that we believers genuinely need one another for the body as a whole to function smoothly. There will be days when the hand will be frustrated with the foot's inability to grasp things as easily as the hand does; but the hand ought not regard the foot as a dispensable impediment. The feet may take the hand to a place where the hand can grasp things better.

The narratives in the book of Acts and the admonitions in the epistles reveal that God values inter-personal harmony more than coming to a certain specific strategy. "They were all in one accord" is often indication that the Holy Spirit was at work in their midst, guiding their discussions and reasoning (cf. Acts 4:24; 5:12; 8:6; 15:24-28; Matt. 18:19-20; Rom. 15:5-6; 1 Cor. 1:10).

This is doubtless part of what Jesus meant when He told His disciples that a call to leadership is a call to service. It is difficult—and more sanctifying—to collaborate with others to form ideas and conclusions and work together for their fulfillment than it is to assess independently the data, form conclusions, and make an argument. Recognize, though, that the latter is the academic enterprise—it is the *modus operandi* of your seminary studies. At the very least, recognize that, upon graduation, you will have more to learn on this score, and that, in this way, your ministry context is a transition from the context of your seminary education.

Your academic training can make you a valuable resource and contributor to your ministry team, or it can make you an obnoxious irritant, even when you are right. How you use the knowledge and skill developed in your academic training is largely a matter of personal maturity. You can discover dangerously low temperatures in seminary, and certainly will in church ministry, but you don't have to be mortally wounded or crippled by spiritual frostbite.

Chapter 5

Humble Service

Serving Others Without It Being a Purely Academic Exercise

We have considered some of the complications and challenges of serving the Lord as one's livelihood. But, of course, serving the Lord means serving people. The correlation of the two is necessary, but it is not always pleasant. Some straight talk is warranted here, in that service to people is too often glamorized and romanticized in sermons, Sunday school lessons, Bible studies, and seminary classrooms.

The Plain Truth about "Serving" in Ministry

A cold, hard fact is that the vast majority of the people to whom you devote your service are undeserving of those services. Your investment of time, attention, energy, and compassion in and for them will probably not pay off (at least not in a way that anyone can see in this life). Some people will stand out as dramatic "fruit of your ministry." But they are the exceptions, not the rule.

Chapter 5

This is exactly what Jesus tried to prepare His twelve disciples for. Serving the Lord is often not very glamorous work; it can often look a lot like washing the dirty feet of people far less gifted and talented than us and who are arguing over which of them is the greatest (John 13:12-17).

Also *other* Christian workers can be a problem. Did you know that the number one reason missionaries are forced to return home from the field is their inability to get along with fellow Christian workers on the field? The stresses and strains of living in close quarters with other people of fervent commitment, along with having to make adjustments to a foreign culture can be too much to bear for many who try it, however well meaning or sincere their original commitment to missions work. Working for God is one thing; working alongside others working for God is another.

This is not just a challenge for missionaries on a foreign field. Wherever you are ministering you must work with other Christians who likewise have leadership gifts and aspirations. One thing about Christians who are committed to doing great things for God is that they have a certain headstrong quality, a tenacity of conviction; this is something that enables them to have such commitment to ministry in the first place. Yet this quality has a downside when it comes to the need to collaborate with others.

True, any form of Christian ministry has its challenges. But serving the Lord means commitment to a life of service, and not just to your ministry "targets" or prospects. Your vision of serving God when you first enter the ministry often just sounds more glamorous and "spiritual" than what it is likely to turn out to be in day-to-day experience.

Jesus told His disciples they did not know what they were getting into (Mark 10:38), but that they would come to understand only after they were into it too deep to get out (John 13:7; cf. Luke 9:62). Perhaps that is also the case with seminarians aspiring to ministry. There is only so much that can be prepared for; some things must simply be learned and accepted through experience itself.

Seminary rightly encourages aspirations to success, dreaming big and attempting great things for God. This is well and good so long as the realities of ministry are recognized and accentuated along the way too. Some disillusionment is probably unavoidable; discouragement at times comes with the territory. (See the section on "disillusionment" in the previous chapter.) Even Jesus Himself expressed frustration (see Matt. 23:37). Many people marveled at His amazing works, but the one time Jesus is said to marvel was when a Gentile centurion expressed greater faith than He had found in all of Israel, the people He was actually trying to reach (Matt. 8:8-13). Jesus invested an enormous amount of His time, energy, attention, and teaching into His "core team," with whom He often was disappointed (see Matt. 14:28-31; 26:36-40; and Mark 4:40-41).

Think of the many people Jesus healed. Think of the investment He poured into His disciples. Yet, when He could have used His friends, colleagues, and beneficiaries of His ministry to rise up and contradict the false accusations brought against Him, He was alone, abandoned to His enemies, convicted, and executed because "they all left Him and fled" (Mark 14:50).

Jesus told us what we can expect when we follow Him in service: "Remember the word that I said to you, 'A slave is not greater than his master.' If they persecuted Me, they will also persecute you; if they kept My word, they will keep yours also. But all these things they will do to you for My name's sake, because they do not know the One who sent Me (John 15:20-21).

Jesus was frustrated and disappointed at the response He received to His service, but He did it anyway.

That is our call, too—to serve anyway, whether we get the recognition we "deserve"; whether our ministries flourish as a result; whether our service results in many lives being transformed. These benefits may or may not happen, but they are not the reason we try to be hospitable, generous, and helpful.

Our motivation must come from something deeper, something greater. Our love for God has to be what underpins our love for people. Our service to people must be viewed as part of our service to God. Otherwise we are destined for disillusionment and burn-out. If we are not careful, our service to people can actually become a manipulative way of "advancing our career."

This is why Jesus emphasized service as an act of *faith*, as evidence of one's trust in God. "Give your gifts in secret," He said, "so that your Father who sees in secret will repay you" (Matt. 6:4). "When you give a luncheon or a dinner, do not invite your friends or your brothers or your relatives or rich neighbors, lest they also invite you in return, and repayment come to you. But when you give a reception, invite the poor, the crippled, the lame, the blind, and you will be blessed, since they do not have the means to repay you; for you will be repaid at the resurrection of the righteous" (Luke 14:12-14).

Service to people may bring with it certain rewards and benefits. A sense of satisfaction comes in seeing someone's life transformed or in seeing someone launch a significant ministry. These are often the motivations for a person entering the ministry, which may not be bad, but which also may be dangerous.

Any motivation short of love for God with an exclusive focus on the Lord's "well done!" will lead to disappointment. The discouragements are just too frequent, the frustrations too common otherwise to keep motivated for service for long.

We do not serve people because they deserve to be served, any more than we are deserving of the service God has rendered to us. Having our love for God as the central motivation for any service leads into several other significant points. Among them, our motivation for studying the Bible needs to be addressed.

The Danger of Studying the Bible for Application

You will hear thousands of times over the course of your life—and if you are a preacher, you may *say* it thousands of times!—that knowledge of the Bible's teaching is not enough; it needs to be *applied* to life. I take the point and affirm it as far as it goes, but, once again, there is a danger here.

True, the Bible needs to be applied and not just memorized; it needs to be heard and read with the full intent of using its principles in one's life and not just "enjoyed." The Bible's principles need to be practiced, not just known in one's head.

So where is the danger in the focus on "application"? The danger lies in overlooking the steps that should take place between knowledge and practice, steps that God Himself upholds as perhaps most important of all.

Compare Deuteronomy 6:6-9 with Proverbs 2:1-5:

> "And these words, which I am commanding you today, shall be on your heart; and you shall teach them diligently to your sons and shall talk of them when you sit in your house and when you walk by the way and when you lie down and when you rise up. And you shall bind them as a sign on your hand

and they shall be as frontals on your forehead. And
you shall write them on the doorposts of your house
and on your gates" (Deut. 6:6-9).

"My son, if you accept my words and store up my
commands within you, turning your ear to wisdom and applying your heart to understanding,
and if you call out for insight and cry aloud for
understanding, and if you look for it as for silver
and search for it as for hidden treasure, then you
will understand the fear of the LORD and find the
knowledge of God" (Prov. 2:1-5).

Several points are worth noting here. First, there is no short-
age of admonition in these passages for us to be diligent, rigorous, and deeply involved in our study of God's Word.

The warnings about accumulating knowledge are not warnings against the accumulation of knowledge itself! Knowledge,
understanding, and wisdom (which go together) are not only
encouraged, but are *demanded* by God's Word, particularly of
those who lead and teach God's people.

Second, though it is clear that the knowledge of God and His
Word is not to remain stuck in our heads without ever making
it beyond the confines of our brains, it is also worth noting that
these passages do not move directly from head to hands, either.
Look at the emphasis of Deuteronomy 6:6, "These words shall
be on your *heart*."

Our study of the Scriptures is to result in character transformation, to mature us in personal and spiritual formation. True,
this could be considered a kind of "application." But it is a different sort of application from what is normally suggested by

the term. Scrutinizing, analyzing, memorizing, and contemplating Scripture is designed by God to reveal His character, and to incite an attraction to that character, so that we, as students of His Word, come to love and embrace *Him* as a *person*—a divine person, yes, but a person.

This increased love of God and God's character, in turn, has a transforming effect. How?

By enabling us to see the goodness of God, the attractiveness of His character, the rightness of His purposes, the trustworthiness and wisdom of His ways, we then also grow more and more to see the worthiness—and *smartness!*—of subjugating every priority in our lives to Him. This recognition of God's goodness and worthiness, beauty, and wisdom needs to take place in us first and then in others, until "the earth shall be filled with the knowledge of the LORD as the waters cover the sea" (Isa. 11:9).

Why should we meditate on God's Word "day and night," as David observed (Ps. 1:2), and why should we consider the Law "sweeter than honey" (Pss. 19:9-10; 119:103)? Because contemplating and meditating on God's Word gives us access to the character and person of God Himself, the one ultimately "behind" the teachings of the Word.

Moses, David, and Solomon (when they were each at their best anyway) are good examples of this point for seminarians, ministers, or would-be ministers, and teachers to contemplate. Like us, their study of God's Word was in part vocationally motivated. In each of their cases, their "job" was to implement the principles of God's Word in the decisions, policies, goals, and objectives for an entire community to adopt and follow. It is easy to get absorbed into and distracted by the challenges, obstacles, and contemplation of the "how-tos" of doing that. In each case, though, they recognized that the study of God's Word was for the purpose of getting to know God, the One behind the "principles" they were contemplating.

When a person studies God's Word with a heart committed to getting to know Him, with a will committed to obeying what He says, a spiritually transformative work happens. This is what Paul meant by having "the mind of Christ" (1 Cor. 2: 16). This means that you begin to think more as Jesus does, to view life with a growing godly wisdom, and to see more clearly what God may be up to in the various challenging circumstances of life.

This is why Proverbs encourages the pursuit of knowledge: "with wisdom, gain understanding" (Prov. 4:5). And this explains why knowledge and wisdom, rightly cultivated, increase one's discernment, prudence, skill, and all that goes with them. Then David was able to say that his study of God's Word had accelerated his maturation process.

"O how I love Thy law! It is my meditation all the day.
Thy commandments make me wiser than my enemies,
for they are ever mine.
I have more insight than all my teachers,
for Thy testimonies are my meditation.
I understand more than the aged,
because I have observed Thy precepts"
(Ps. 119:97-100, emphases added).

Observe the increase in character and spiritual formation thus brought about, as well: "I have restrained my feet from every evil way, that I may keep Thy word. I have not turned aside from Thine ordinances, for You Yourself have taught me" (Ps. 119:101-102).

Rigorous, concentrated study of God's Word is a good thing. It is not an end in itself, but neither is the end entirely the "practical application" to one's own or another person's life. Part of the purpose of God's Word is to stimulate and cultivate one's understanding of and love for God Himself. When this happens, our hearts are transformed, our characters are transformed, our entire outlook is transformed, made more mature, made more wise, and is more in accord with God's goals and purposes.

Having undergone this process, one becomes a better leader, a better minister, a better pastor, or a better teacher. But that is actually just a fringe benefit of a far more important transformative work of the Spirit in all this.

When "Knowledge" Is a Tool of One's Trade

As noted so far, the biblically prescribed purpose of knowledge is first and foremost the cultivation of our understanding of and relationship with God, which in turn produces transformation of our heart, mind, will, soul, and character. Effective ministry proceeds from a heart already right with God, much as good fruit is produced from a healthy tree (Luke 6:43-45).

In many ways your ministry as a vocation can be detrimental to your faith, your walk with God, or your spiritual health, perhaps even your mental health! People can go into the ministry for the wrong reasons: as an act of penance or in return for God's doing them some service; as a means of trying to invigorate a flagging spiritual life; to advance in one's spiritual growth; or even because they were browbeaten into it by some sermon or well-meaning family member or friend, and various other unworthy motivations.

This section focuses on those who have legitimately sensed God's call to pursue professional, vocational ministry. The education, knowledge accumulation, and professional development usually required of such persons carries with it some liabilities, dangers, and mixed motives needing transformation.

Pride, Arrogance, and Hubris

"Pride" is a character deficiency that involves thinking of yourself more highly than you ought to think or having a desire to be regarded by others as superior, which motivates your actions, attitudes, and aspirations. "Arrogance" is what results when a proud person comes to enjoy some success from his or her efforts. Psychologists note that "pride" often stems from insecurity. But that does not excuse the problem. And "hubris" describes what characterizes the presumptuous attitudes and actions of the proud, arrogant person over time—with connotations of setting up such a person for his or her eventual, inevitable fall.

As noted in our earlier chapters, "knowledge puffs up" (1 Cor. 8:1 Niv). This is true in any field, secular or sacred. You may easily think of individuals who match the phrase, "arrogant doctor," "arrogant professor," or "arrogant musician."

But the phrase "arrogant pastor" or "arrogant minister" is a different matter. A vocation that is supposed to be devoted to the forwarding of the (spiritual) success of others does not fit well with the self-awareness, self-congratulation, and self-promotion connoted by the term "arrogant."

Ministers are not immune to the seduction of pride, much less professional Bible or theology teachers. There is a real rush that comes with being the one people look to for biblical answers, theological insight, relational counsel, problem solving, organizational leadership, and/or the casting of vision for a local congregation.

How many seminarians pursue the ministry as a vocation imagining that their outcome will be like Solomon's wise administration of Israel? Yes, the workload is heavy, the challenges are great, and one bears all the responsibilities of whatever corner of the Kingdom one may be leading. On the other hand, imagine the perks of being the Solomon of 1 Kings 10:1-10, with the queen of Sheba rendered "breathless" at Solomon's wisdom and his administration of so impressive a regime.

It is a wonderful thing to be used of the Lord. There are few things in life more gratifying than working toward (or better yet, leading people to) the success of some goal for which God has given you a passion. However, all this carries an occupational hazard. With each aspiration, the temptation arises to imagine oneself as "the key" to it all. With each success comes the temptation of believing the press reports about oneself, or worse, to desire the kind of praise and honor that belongs only to God.

Seen in this light, it is not surprising that the attention and commendations Solomon received from the Queen of Sheba (1 Kings 10:1-10) eventually degenerated years later into King Hezekiah showing off his wealth to those who had come to see him from a land far way (2 Kings 20:13-23). What took a few generations in this instance can happen within a single lifetime. The king who inherited the Solomonic treasures just could not resist showing off all the gold and precious stones and treasures and the abundance of spices with which the Lord had blessed him and his kingdom to people who had come to see him from Babylon, a land far away. Hezekiah could not resist the urge to impress them with all his successes, accomplishments, honors, and rewards. And impress them he did.

The Lord, however, is always displeased at such displays of hubris, even if the rewards and honors were well earned, and even if He Himself was originally behind the honors. The purpose of God's bestowing such honors is to foster appreciation and love for Him, not to elevate the individual.

God sent Isaiah the prophet to tell him, "Hear the word of the LORD. 'Behold, the days are coming when all that is in your house, and all that your fathers have laid up in store to this day shall be carried to Babylon; nothing shall be left. And some of your sons who shall issue from you, whom you shall beget, shall be taken away; and they shall become officials in the palace of the king of Babylon'" (2 Kings 20:16-18).

This point is made frequently in Scripture.

"The fear of the LORD is to hate evil, pride and arrogance and the evil way" (Prov. 8:13).

"When pride comes, then comes dishonor, But with the humble is wisdom" (Prov. 11:2).

"Pride goes before destruction, and a haughty spirit before stumbling" (Prov. 16:18).

"A man's pride will bring him low, but a humble spirit will obtain honor" (Prov. 29:23).

And perhaps most important of all, the point that underpins all these others is James's words:

"God is opposed to the proud, but gives grace to the humble. Submit therefore to God" (James 4:6-7).

Peter repeated this truth in 1 Peter 5:5-6:

"God is opposed to the proud, but gives grace to the humble.
Therefore, humble yourselves under the mighty hand of God,
that He may exalt you at the proper time."

Face this squarely: seminary may not help you develop resistance to these temptations and penchants. In fact in some ways seminary can make it worse.

Seminary is a unique environment, and a somewhat artificial measure of ministerial giftedness too. Academic institutions can measure and assess only certain kinds of giftedness or achievement, and they are often not the same set of qualities necessary for successful ministry. Your research is scrutinized carefully and assessments officially registered. Of course, measurements are necessary and need to be objective, and objective assessments can measure only certain areas of tangible, demonstrable achievement. Grading systems need not be eradicated, but their limitations need to be recognized.

In academic settings, the "brightest" are rewarded and heralded as "the best." While to recognize accomplishments and giving honor to whom it is due is commendable, the dynamic of grading and academic rewards can foster some unhealthy attitudes and habits of mind and heart. One can be motivated by the earning of the grade, the prospect of reward, and the praise of people one respects. These dangerous motivations need to be checked by the higher motivation to please God alone.

Furthermore knowledge accumulation and the ability to cite facts and develop insightful theses are the primary means of earning reward in an academic setting. One who grows overly accustomed to earning reward for these things can come to value too highly the mere mastery of concepts, the formulation of ideas.

All the entanglements and tripwires of pride, arrogance, vanity, disillusionment, and misguided achievement can be avoided by making love for God your central motivation, and pleasing God the goal for whatever service you are engaged in. "Joining the service" is not just for military personnel; it is actually a phrase more apt for those entering the ministry.

Pursuing a career in academics (teaching the Bible, theology, church history, Christian education, missions, pastoral ministry, or organizational leadership) is a subcategory of ministry. Academic ministry is ministry, and all ministry means service— service to God through service to others.

Balancing Academics with Service

One way to keep from growing cold or stale in your seminary studies is to engage in various forms of non-academic service. Here is a brief starter list of ideas in no particular order. If these ideas spark other ideas you would rather do, then do those. Let the Lord prompt you. You may well learn about your deeper heart motives in these non-academic settings.

- Volunteer to help in the church nursery (more advanced: during the Christmas or Christmas Eve service).

- Do some of your preaching or teaching in a nursing home; no honorariums allowed! (even better, when you are finished preaching, visit some of the bedridden).

- Visit people from your church who have been hospitalized (even better, while there, be alert for or ask the nursing staff if there are people in other rooms who could use a visitor or someone to pray with them).

- Be part of any ministry-service team at your church (this can be strictly on an "as needed," or "as available" basis)— elderly home service; home repair for the needy; food distribution; blanket or clothing distribution).

- Go with a friend or family member into the city and distribute some of your unused coats or blankets; or look for people for whom you could buy a meal or cup of coffee—look them in the eye and talk with them; offer to pray with them.

- Help in a soup kitchen or homeless shelter ministry.

- Participate in a "learn to read" or "English as second language" program in the community.

A Final Word

"Let not many of you become teachers, my brethren, knowing that as such we shall incur a stricter judgment" (James 3:1).

I hope James' warning scares you at least a little; that it sends at least a little chill up your spine. If it does not, let me urge you not to go into teaching or preaching as your vocation.

For those of you who read James 3:1 and gulp, but are compelled to charge on in the calling to teach or preach or seek leadership in ministry because you can do nothing else, let me urge you to pause just a moment longer to think about this.

The calling you believe you have been given is a serious one and a high one. But know this: there are easier livelihoods. With the talents, skills, and capabilities you have, you could make more money doing something else.

The ministry is a busy life. It includes all the stresses of a "normal job," but it also adds stresses and strains, the needs and expectations of other people. Know what you are getting into. Enter the ministry with your eyes wide open to what you are agreeing to and committing to before the Lord.

Yet there is no better life. At times you will be disappointed, frustrated, and discouraged; but even in the midst of this you can enjoy the Lord's blessings. At times you may feel like people are hurling insults. And they will. Any minister, teacher, or leader of God's people will experience dark moments. But there are also times when you can just feel the warmth of Jesus' smile as you engage in your feeble efforts to work for Him. However feeble, you can say from your heart that you are trying your best to serve Him faithfully.

Some of us will work in fields of hard ground, mostly digging weeds. Most of us get a chance to see some fruit, though; and sometimes that fruit is dramatic, and you know the supernatural work of the Spirit is involved because it far exceeds any contribution you made in the person's life. After a few years, almost every pastor or teacher can see God's hand at work in people's lives and can enjoy a sense of godly pride and gratification for what God has done. These are blessings from the Father that one can receive in few other lines of work.

Do not come into the field of ministry if you are not prepared to work hard, for low pay, with great patience, and no guarantee of seeing visible fruit in this life. A lot of work remains to be done, though; much planting, much weeding, much fertilizing and, Lord willing, much harvesting too. If God has called you to it, great! Put your hand to the plow, and do not look back.

Chapter 6

Family and Friends

How Relationships Can Keep You Grounded and Encouraged

In this volume we have emphasized authentic relationships as an important part of seminary education. The dangers of privatization, isolation, and individualization are always lurking. You need to know and be known by trusted comrades as you embark on an advanced study of our Creator and His revelation. Two of the key people groups who can help you in this endeavor are family members and friends.

When we go hiking, most of us easily recall the advice of a Boy Scout or Girl Scout leader: "Never hike alone; always take someone with you!" Aron Ralston ignored this warning.

In 2003, Ralston embarked on a hiking trip in Utah's Blue John Canyon. A boulder dislodged and crushed his right forearm and trapped him against the canyon wall. Ralston did not tell anyone of his hiking plans before he set out and he thought no one would be looking for him even if he was late in returning home. After he was trapped, Ralston thought he would die in the canyon. He spent five excruciating days slowly sipping his small amount of remaining water while trying to extricate his arm and maintain consciousness. After amputating his own right arm, he stumbled out of the canyon and found some hikers who helped him find assistance. The amazing incident was documented in Ralston's amazing autobiography *Between a Rock and a Hard Place*[1] and was the subject of the 2010 film, *127 Hours*

Embarking on an advanced study of God and the Bible is a little like hiking in the mountains. We should prepare for the journey with much preplanning. A clear destination should be marked out and we should never isolate ourselves from others. The importance of staying grounded through the advice and encouragement of faithful friends and family members cannot be overemphasized. Isolation and a "going it alone" mentality can quickly creep in and become enemies of advanced ministerial and theological training.

Family Members

The student who endeavors to study theology and Christianity usually receives a range of responses from close family members. At one extreme are family members who strongly encourage this kind of study and pursuit of God. A close or extended family member may say, "I always knew you would go into the ministry. Your grandfather was a preacher, and your mom always told me she thought you had a special calling on your life."

At the other extreme are family members who feel the need to tell you what a huge mistake you are making with your life. A relative may respond, "Theology? What a waste of time and

---

1   Aron Ralston, *Between a Rock and a Hard Place* (New York: Atria Books, 2004).

talent. You need to go into a practical field of work like sales or marketing." I have heard both of these kinds of comments on numerous occasions by students who tell me why they decided to tackle a seminary education.

Both of these extremes can be damaging. In the first instance the counselors are laying out expectations that the family member may or may not be willing or eager to uphold. In the second case the advice received can be discouraging, almost disheartening. When a student operates without the blessing of close family members, especially one's parents, the times of doubt and discouragement, which inevitably will arrive, may feel like an almost unbearable weight.

Jesus endured this kind of advice from family members. They actually called Him crazy. Matthew records a family incident. "While He was still speaking to the crowds, behold, His mother and brothers were standing outside, seeking to speak to Him" (Matt. 12:46). If we did not know the end of the story, we might wonder what these family members were saying to Him. You might expect one of them to say, "Jesus, you are doing amazing work!" Or another might have responded, "Jesus, you are making our family proud. Everyone back home is rejoicing over Your newfound fame."

But, that is not how they responded. Mark relayed another time of family involvement; "When His own people [family] heard of this [Jesus drawing crowds and casting out demons], they went out to take custody of [arrest] Him; for they were saying, 'He has lost His senses'" (Mark 3:21). Jesus had to put up with the Pharisees, the Sadducees, the scribes, the doubters, the doomsayers, and even his own family members. All were accusing Him of being crazy. You may hear the same thing from some close family members.

Instead of overreacting you need to be prepared for both of these extreme responses (praise and ridicule) as you begin your theological training. Be cautious about wearing the mantle of a previous family member. Even though your grandfather or great-grandfather was a missionary, that does not necessarily mean you are to do the same. You may be, and you could be quite effective. But you need not assume or feel obligated to fulfill a family role that is handed down to you.

On the other hand you may be one of the first in your recent family history to embrace Christ and the gospel message and to be called to the ministry. You will need to be sensitive to the doubts and disbeliefs of those who do not yet hold the same faith commitments you have. To them, embarking on a multi-year study of an ancient book (the Bible) and a religious teacher (Jesus of Nazareth) does indeed seem foolish. To them it may appear you have fallen into the hands of a cult or strange religious group. They may reason that you should be studying something practical.

Spiritual Friendship

Fortunately family members are not the only source of encouragement and advice on your spiritual journey. Obviously the gift of the Holy Spirit poured out on Jesus' followers on the Day of Pentecost changed everything. Up to that point the Holy Spirit was described as coming on someone or as temporarily filling a person marked out for special ministry. But after Pentecost the Holy Spirit permanently filled the believers in Jesus Christ, which still happens today.

Fellow Christians who study along with you will in many ways become like new family members. You will meet brothers and sisters in Christ who share the same longings and desires you now share. This can be an exciting time to learn you are not alone on this journey of discovering more about God. Throughout the life of the church, Christ-followers embarking on a deeper study of God, have found solace in what can best be described as *spiritual friendship*.[2] Today we may use a term like "accountability" or a phrase like "prayer partner."

David Benner defines spiritual friendship as "a gift of hospitality, presence and dialogue" shown from one person to another.[3] Other phrases for this unique relationship are "soul hospitality" and "faithful friends." The point here is that you need to be both open *and* intentional about receiving such friends. God may bless you with a spiritual friendship that will help you in your darkest times of doubt and your greatest moments of celebration.

How Family and Friends Can Help Keep Us Grounded

A certain phone company was successful in signing up new customers for their long-distance plan by advertising a program designed to reach out to family and friends. Some loved this new approach and quickly recruited acquaintances and co-workers in order to save money on their phone bills. Others loathed the

---

2   *De spiritali amicitia* ("On Spiritual Friendship") is the most well-known work on this subject. This book was penned in 1160 by Aelred, who served as the abbot of Rievaulx until his death on January 12, 1167. *Aelred of Rievaulx: Spiritual Friendship,* trans. Lawrence Braceland, ed. Marsha L. Dutton, (Collegeville, MN: Cistercian Publications, 2010).

3   David G. Benner, *Sacred Companions* (Downers Grove, IL: InterVarsity Press, 2002), 46.

idea that they would be asked to use close friends and members of their own family as commodities for price lowering. Neither approach was morally wrong; they were simply two different ways of viewing a discount promotion.

However, once you have determined to set out on your journey of discovering more about who God is and how He operates in the world, it is important to remember who you are. In other words, it is helpful to analyze what you inherited from your family and learned from your friends.

During upcoming times of critical thinking and deep analysis of who God is, we need to remember that He is the Creator and we are the created. Don't fall into the trap of reversing those roles or blurring the distinctions. God created you from a specific set of humans in a specific location at a predetermined time in history.

This unique aspect of who you are (and who you are not) needs to be celebrated. You are limited in your knowledge; but God is not. You can be in only one place at a time; He is everywhere at once. You are fallible and prone to sin; He is holy and without sin. You and I continually make mistakes; He never has and never will. Your family of origin speaks volumes about how you will go about comprehending and understanding God. This connection to living and learning may not be so readily apparent at first.

Think of two potential family scenarios. The Johnsons can best be described as a tightly straight laced group of folks. The father and mother both operated within highly controlled boundaries and often pushed their children to excel in sports and academics. To the Johnsons, esoteric discussions that were not practical or questions without correct answers were seen as giant time-wasters. As for church selection, the Johnsons preferred worshiping within the faithful liturgical structures in which they had been raised. To them, God could be explained and defined by the catechesis of their forefathers.

The Robinsons, on the other hand, were open to novel ideas about God. They enjoyed late-night discussions and weekend retreats on philosophical topics. The Robinsons would stay at one church for a good number of years, but felt no remorse about following the leading of the Lord when new worship opportunities in their town became available. They felt little tension living with the uncertainties that life often presents, choosing to believe that all of life is an open-ended journey.

Can you see how a person growing up in one of these two families might initially approach the discipline of theological higher education? A student from the Johnson family may approach her studies hoping to confirm (or confront) the right answers she received from her parents and church. The student from this family may initially feel uncomfortable being asked to critically analyze their closely held beliefs. On the other hand, someone from the extended Johnson family might express shock and disappointment if they learned a close relative was wrestling with a traditional approach the Johnson family took toward worship or belief about God.

Someone raised in the Robinson family may feel constricted by an in-depth study of the creeds and catechisms of the faith. A Robinson family member may be surprised to learn that so much theology has already been systematized into a coherent set of assertions and propositions. Coming into their theological training with a desire for wide-open debate and endless exploration may be a shock to a Robinson, who quickly realizes that countless hours will be devoted to memorizing Greek and Hebrew paradigms, learning which church councils settled which

Christian heresies, and understanding the precise argument for each book of the Bible.

Again, knowing your family of origin can help keep you grounded and balanced in your seminary studies. The Reformation theologian John Calvin proposed that we embark on not only knowledge of God but also that we engage in a vigorous search for "double-knowledge"—knowing about God, and also knowing oneself.[4] At first a search for self-knowledge or self-understanding may sound like pride. We have been taught with good intention that the Christian life involves service toward others, a focus on the world's needs and not our own, and "forgetting what lies behind" (Phil. 3:13).

However, this does not mean we should avoid an honest evaluation of how God has created us and wired us for service. A mark of maturity is being aware of our own temperament, gifts, talents, abilities, and habits of relating with others. Even the apostle Paul, who encouraged his readers to "press on," did not mean we should never recall our past experiences; all of which work together to mold and shape us into who and what we are today. Paul recalled for his readers how he had been schooled by Gamaliel, how he had persecuted and killed Christians, and how he was anxiously climbing up the ranks of Jewish teachers seeking a place of prominence.

But when he encouraged us to "forget what lies behind," he meant that we are no longer to live in such a way that the sins and mistakes of the past hold us back from doing all that God asks of us. We are to press on in our Christian walk and not let

---

4   John Calvin, *Institutes of the Christian Religion*, The Library of Christian Classics, ed. John T. McNeill, trans. Ford Lewis Battles (Philadelphia: Westminster Press, 1960), I.i.1

the shackles of painful memories keep us imprisoned in a sea of doubt and discouragement.

So, taking time to understand who we are and where we have come from (our family of origin and all that that involves) is actually a humble endeavor that stands us in good stead as we embark on knowing more about God. And in addition to our family of origin it is important to recognize the "faith family" or religious environment in which we have been nurtured to this point in our faith journey. Understanding the vast differences in the body of Christ is a mark of spiritual maturity.

Staying Grounded

I (Paul) remember when I studied at a Bible college for the first time. Everything was so new and fresh. The insights were amazing. It was like an ongoing, daily Bible study. The professors seemed like infallible giants of the faith. I was making amazing strides in my knowledge about the Bible, God, the church, the history of Christianity, and other aspects of ministry. And when I returned home, I subtly let others know what I was learning. I did not think I was being arrogant, but after looking back on that, I'm surprised that a few close family members and friends did not say to my face what they were undoubtedly saying behind my back, *"Wow, has this guy changed for the worse!"*

I am thankful I can laugh about it now, but we need to recognize that pride can creep into our lives when we begin to think we know a little more about the Bible than others do. Pride may set in when we project our knowledge onto others in an attempt to "help" them see the errors of their ways. Old friends, who know us well, can help keep us humble if we are open to their rebuke. Family members, who were with us when we knew very little, should be able to tell us if we are fouling the air with our self-importance.

If you are open to their prompting, your family members and friends can be used by God to help keep you grounded. Be aware that knowledge acquisition, as helpful as it is, can lead to over-inflated egos and feelings of self-importance. It is truly an oxymoron when you think about it. We are endeavoring to learn about our Savior who came to serve. We want to know more about how Jesus emptied Himself and gave Himself up for us. We are being trained in how to serve with humility and lowliness of heart. But yet once we feel we know a little about all of this, we become puffed up with pride.

On our seminary's campus (Dallas Theological Seminary) stands a statue of Jesus washing Peter's feet. When my children were much younger, they used to love running to the statue and climbing on it. One of them would inevitably announce, "I'm standing on Peter!" But actually they would be on Jesus' shoulders. Many people think that Peter should have been washing the feet of Jesus. Jesus was divine; Peter was not. Jesus already knew and understood the lessons of humility and service; Peter did not. Thus one would think that Jesus would have His own feet washed. And yet Jesus was the one doing the washing. He was showing Peter that as followers of Christ, pride is to have no place in our lives.

The faithful assistance of family and friends can be helpful. They are the ones who knew us "back then," when we had very little knowledge of theology or doctrine. God uses reminders in our lives to show us that our learning and growing in Him is His work and not our own.

We also need to remember that there are many different gifts in the body of Christ. We do not all possess the same gift or passion. You are one small part of a great whole. You are one aspect of what God is doing in His work in the world.

How Family and Friends Can Keep You Encouraged

Family and friends can help knock pride and arrogance out of your life if you are open and humble to receiving their rebukes. But the reverse is also true. Family and friends can be a trusted source of timely encouragement as well. Just as they "knew you when" and thus are able to keep your ego in check, they can remind you that "you can do it!"

God will bring into your life friends whom you need to help you accomplish your seminary training. Old friends who know you well and new friends whom you will meet along the way will help you see that you are not forgotten on this God-called journey. You can lean into the comforting presence of the divine Counselor; the Holy Spirit. But you can also partner with likeminded friends and mentors who have your best interests at heart. The voice of encouragement can become for you like a drink of water on a scorching hot day. A proverb reminds us, "Like apples of gold in settings of silver is a word spoken in right circumstances" (Prov. 25:11).

When David was on the run from King Saul, he found the strength to follow the advice of his good friend. Learning of his father's attempt to kill David, "Jonathan, Saul's son, arose and went to David at Horesh, and encouraged him [lit., 'strengthened his hand'] in God" (1 Sam. 23:16). You will be blessed indeed if God brings into your life a friend like Jonathan who is committed to your welfare. And you can be a friend like Jonathan to another student whom you sense needs a word of encouragement.

Some of these new friends whom God brings into your life may hold values different from yours. You may be reluctant to reach out to someone who differs from you, comes from a different part of the world, or has a different background than you have. And yet, he may end up being the very person God uses to encourage you when you are "down." Are you open and willing to receive whomever God might bring into your life for such ministry refreshment? And are you willing to reach out to another fellow student whom you sense may need a timely word of assistance. Not all will receive what you offer, but some will. And a select few could become long-time faithful friends.

I am thankful that several of my professors encouraged me to try new activities and skills, leaving the results to God. I was taught that believers would provide plenty of feedback on whether my ministry endeavors were fruitful or fateful.

Jesus, Friend of Sinners

God blesses the balanced. He wants you to keep academics and godly living in balance. And family and friends can help you do that. As limited, finite creatures we must remember that it is impossible to know, do, and be all that God desires for us. We have a limited amount of knowledge and limited resources. We will face problems and trials. And so we need to hold onto our identity as those who have died with Christ.

On the cross, Jesus died for frail, helpless creatures like us, people who can no more help themselves than a fish can live without water. We enter our seminary training as limited, finite creatures. We will fail. We will fall. We will flunk an exam. We will write a poor paper. We will preach a boring, confusing sermon. We will counsel someone with unhealthy advice. However, the grace of God calls us not to perfection but to effectiveness. The cross does not disqualify us from ministry; it qualifies us to serve.

Family and friends can help keep you humble. So look to them for encouragement. They can strengthen your soul with timely, warm, God-given wisdom. This will keep you going. But above all, keep your eyes fixed on Jesus, the starter and finisher, the beginning and the end, the Alpha and the Omega of your faith. He will never fail. Jesus will never leave you nor forsake you. He will be your faithful friend to the end.

So carry on in your seminary studies as you prepare for a lifetime of fruitful, faithful service. Keep academics and spirituality, study, and godliness in balance. Why? Because blessed are the balanced!